GOSPEL MUSIC

An African American Art Form

Dr. Joan Rucker-Hillsman

FriesenPress

Suite 300 – 990 Fort Street
Victoria, BC, Canada V8V 3K2
www.friesenpress.com

Foreword: Dr. James Boyer for the late Dr. Horace Boyer
Editor: Dominique Lloyd

Special thanks are extended to family, friends, colleagues, and
supporters of this project on Gospel Music.

ISBN
978-1-4602-3219-4 (Hardcover)
978-1-4602-3220-0 (Paperback)
978-1-4602-3221-7 (eBook)

1. Music, Religious, Gospel

Distributed to the trade by The Ingram Book Company

Table of Contents

Dedication

This book is dedicated to the memory and contributions of the pioneers of gospel music who paved the way for the success of current artists in the field.

In Loving memory of my father, William Isaiah Rucker, a young quartet singer, who was killed in World War II at a young age.

Special love is extended to my colleagues and especially to my beloved family, who has been the "wind beneath my wings", always encouraging me in my many endeavors (My mother, the late Elizabeth Gilliard Rucker, my husband, scientist, genius in the field of engineering/computer science, politician, and founder of "World Christian Church" in Suitland, Maryland, Howard University graduate, none other than the late Rev. Horace Hillsman of Atlanta, Georgia, who also served as a junior ambassador for the late Dr. Martin Luther King, Jr. And to my son Quentin Hillsman an author, music artist and currently the head coach of Syracuse University's Woman's Basketball Team.

Acknowledgments

Gratitude is extended to my colleagues, students, friends and supporters for this project on Gospel music which is an invaluable resource for those in studying the concept of gospel. Special thanks are also extended to individuals in the interviews for my previous publications as well as this one. Dr. E. Myron Noble, Mid-Atlantic Regional Press was the publisher for my first edition. Dionne Warwicke wrote the Forward to the book. Special thanks are also extended to my Gospel Music Workshop of America (GMWA) family, Rev. James Cleveland, Founder, of which I have been affiliated since its inception, currently on the Academic administrative staff, National Collegiate Chair (Gospel Goes to College) in the Academic Division and on the National Board of Directors, Bishop Albert Jamison, Chairman of the Board of Directors.

I would also like to mention the late Mancel "Speedy" Warrick (Gospel Promoter and the father of Dionne and Dee Dee), who gave me the opportunity to work in the recording field, along with the late Anthony Manno, for the publication of our first book, The Progress of Gospel Music. These co-authors inspired me to continue my writings and research on the cultural heritage of gospel music as an art form.

Thanks to Dr. Judith McAllister, National Recording Artist, for her encouraging comments on gospel. She stated, " the evolution and progress of gospel music-from the Negro Spirituals of our fore-fathers-has been the ship by which we as a people have traversed through the struggles of our lives and set in our sight the hope for a better day."

Appreciation extended to all of my supporters, including my technical editor R. Dominic Lloyd, graduate of Syracuse University creative writing department and Michelle Brooks, graduate of Bowie State University, my former office assistant, and to my son Quentin Hillsman and family.

Finally, to Dr. James Boyer and his family for sharing valuable information and inspiration from contributions of his brother, the late Dr. Horace Boyer, who wrote the Foreword to the first edition of this book. This powerful message (Foreword) is reprinted in this current revision as a legacy tribute to him. Dr. James and Dr. Horace Boyer are historically known as "The Boyer Brothers." Together they made great contributions as performers and historians of Gospel Music.

Foreword

By Professor Horace C. Boyer

This Foreword was published in a revised edition in 1998. Dr. Boyer died in 1909. He committed his life toward mainstreaming gospel music and making it a legitimate part of higher education, states his brother, Dr. James Boyer, a prominent authority on gospel music. I am proud to share this foreword with the readers in this newly revised edition of "Gospel Music: An African American Art Form." It reads as follows:

With the Emancipation Proclamation (1863) and the ratification of the Thirteenth Amendment (1865), millions of former slaves were free to, as they believed; make sole and final decisions about their lives. Not least among the decisions they had to make was what kind of music would best complement their religious services, now that they were free to worship when, wherever, and as they desired.

This was not an easy task, for in two hundred and twenty-five (225) years of slavery they had amassed a hefty catalogue of sacred songs. They had the psalms of the seventeenth century; the lining hymns of the eighteenth century, and the camp meeting spirituals, Negro Spirituals, and shape note songs of the nineteenth century. Yet none of these seemed appropriate for their new found freedom and the tremendous migration and would occupy them for the next seventy (70) years. Negro Spirituals, the beloved music of the slave era, gradually lost popularity in church services but was rescued by such college groups as the Fisk, Hampton, and Tuskegee Jubilee Singers. Black ministers encouraged the singing of the relatively new gospel hymns composed by such white composers as William Batchelder Bradbury (1816-68), Philip Paul Bliss (1838-76), and Ira David Sankey (1840-1908). The newly established mid-week service was the only occasion where church members could sing songs of their own composition.

Though it would be a quarter of a century before they knew it, Black church members were rescued on April 9, 1906 when Jennie Evans (1893-1936) "spoke in tongues" and signaled the founding of the African American Pentecostal movement, the Azusa Street Movement (Revival) Lasting from 1903-1906, inspired by the founding of Black Pentecostal churches throughout the United States and introduced "sanctified" singing. Characterized by high energy, singing at the extremes of ranges, inserting "fill-in" words where rests would ordinarily be observed, and featuring the leader over the congregation, this new music captivated the Black church in the United States. While the Baptists and Methodists were hesitant to adopt the music, they nonetheless seized every opportunity to hear it.

Separate and apart from "sanctified" singing, in 1915 a group of men working in the mines in Tuscaloosa, Alabama, under the direction of R. C. Foster (b. 1899), formed a quartet, patterning themselves after the famous Fisk Jubilee Singers, and began singing Negro Spirituals and harmonized versions of the gospel hymns of Bradbury and Sankey, among other composers. It was not long before they began to adopt some of the techniques of the "sanctified" singers and the age of the "Jubilee" quartet was born. Within a decade, a group of blind singers, accompanying themselves on guitars, began singing this new music. It was almost impossible to avoid the sounds of "sanctified" singing, either highly energetic or well modulated, in Black communities throughout the United States.

Recognizing the influence of the music, as well as the desire of choirs and soloist to sing it, the National Baptist Convention, the largest organization of Black Christians in the United States, finally caved in and in 1921 published Gospel Pearls, the first collection of songs that were to be sung in the new style. Containing songs by many of the white gospel hymn composers, the collection introduced a number of Black gospel song composers who would yield a great influence on African American gospel music. Among these were Charles Albert Tindley (1851-1933), composer of "We'll Understand It Better By and By"; Charles Price Jones (1865-1949), who composed "I'm Happy With Jesus Alone"; Lucie Eddie Campbell (1885-1963) whose "He'll Understand," and Say "Well Done" is a Gospel standard, and Thomas Andrew Dorsey (1899-1993), who penned "Precious Lord, Take My Hand," organized the first gospel choir in 1932, and who, rightfully so, became known as the "Father" of African American gospel music.

Within twenty (20) years of its publication, Gospel Pearls, and a dynasty of publishing houses in Chicago whose sole inventory was Black gospel, was supplying gospel music to every state in the union. A group of gospel singers led by Singer Rosetta Tharpe (1915-73), Mahalia Jackson

(1911-72), Clara Ward (1924-73) Ira Tucker (b.1923) and the Dixie Hummingbirds, Sam Cooke (1931-64) and the Soul Stirrers, James Cleveland (1931-91), Edwin Hawkins (b.1943) and Kirk Franklin (b.1970), in a short fifty (50) years, made African American gospel music the most arresting music of the last half of the twentieth century. And, scholars began to write books about the music; it moved to Broadway and into the movies; it moved into all denominations of churches, and FINALLY, into American schools. There was only one question left to be answered. How can this music be taught?

While Dr. Joan R. Hillsman's book provides history, biography, analysis, and repertoire, the jewel in the crown is the section teaching materials and methods: the mini lesson plans. Even the most inexperienced teacher will find the resources here to conduct classes in the history, analysis, and even the performance of gospel music with confidence and enjoyment. In the words of a song recorded by Clara Ward "Who Could Ask For Anything More?"

Enjoy this treasure, learn it, and teach it with joy.

Horace Clarence Boyer

Horace Clarence Boyer
Professor of Music, University of
Massachusetts at Amherst and author of
How Sweet The Sound-The Golden Age of Gospel (1995)

Preface

This book is designed for the general reader of gospel music as well as for those who incorporate gospel into their lesson plans on the academic level. "Gospel Music: An African American Art Form" provides basic information on the heritage of gospel from its African roots, Negro Spirituals, traditional and contemporary gospel music trends. The mission and purpose statement of this book is to provide a framework of study of gospel music which is the mainstream of other music genres.

There are eight detailed sections, appendices and various resources on gospel music that are included. The first section (1), "African Roots and Characteristics" highlights the origin and development of the Negro Spiritual. Section two (2), "The Spiritual Movement" and its origin and development gives an account of the genre of decoding the spirituals, preservation, Spirituals in the Civil Rights Movement, The Fisk Jubilee Singers and musical selections. Section three (3), "Black Congregational Singing" expounds on some of the informal styles used in worship services that may be prevalent in some predominantly Black churches.

Many of the styles have been replaced with standard contemporary genres. Section four (4), "The Gospel Movement" provides a historical survey, time-line of the music, toward a definition, and the progress of gospel. It also cites forms of African American music styles that have impacted upon gospel music as a fusion. Section five (5) refers to "The Gripping" and lasting stylistic effect that gospel has embedded in the performance of R&B and Cross-over artists. Section six (6), "Youth in Gospel", provides a youthful perspective in the new millennium. Section seven (7), "Gospel: A Part of the Curriculum", is most valuable, especially to those who include gospel music in an academic setting. Lastly, Section eight (8) provides details for creating lesson plans and giving suggestions of many things to do in the classroom, curriculum ideas, and activities to enhance learning. Overall, this book is a valuable resource for providing a wealth of knowledge of the cultural heritage of "Gospel music as an art form". It should be shared with all cultures. Read it, enjoy it!

I. AFRICAN ROOTS

Music in African Life

The music of the Black man has its roots in his homeland, Africa. In all parts of Africa, music is an integral part of daily living. In the Western world, although music is quite essential, it is often looked upon as an added luxury. In Africa, music is a process of living. Music is ever present before birth, after birth and beyond death. There are certain rituals to commemorate each milestone in ones life. These traditions are celebrated by the villagers as they join in singing and dancing for such occasions as, the naming of the child, when a child cuts his first tooth, at puberty, circumcision rites for boys, womanhood, marriages and burials, only to name a few. Music for other occasions may be performed for wars, festivals, political ceremonies, battles, seasonal and special events. In summary, music and dance go hand-n-hand, and African communities feel free to incorporate these as needed for various occasions.

An interview with a presiding Elder at The Church of Pentecost in Syracuse, Nick Adjeibadi from Ghana, West Africa, confirmed that African music permeates all aspects of daily life. The church has nine nationalities working within the congregation under one common bond. Some of the parishioners are from Haiti, Ghana, Nigeria, Sierra Leone, and Ivory Coast.

Adjeibadi, returning from their Sunday worship service and dressed elegantly in their native garb, stated that their religious celebration in worship consists of dancing, clapping, tapping, drumming, and praises.

African American Music Characteristics

African American Music, often referred to as Afro-American music, consists of all music of African descent: spirituals, blues, rhythm and blues, ragtime, jazz, gospel, rap, hip-hop, and other emerging forms by Africans and African Americans in the diaspora. (See definitions in Gospel Fusions section). African American music has played a vital role in shaping, contributing, and influencing the development of almost all music world-wide. In classical music some composers incorporated Black thematic materials into their larger works. In the diaspora various fusions and blends may be evident in music compositions.

Throughout all African American music, the characteristics such as syncopation, cross-rhythms, call and response, improvisation and other African elements of music are infiltrated. These elements will, perhaps, be present in music throughout the coming decades. General descriptions of these elements may be cited as:

- **Syncopation**- Placing the accents on beats where it would not normally occur.

- **Cross-Rhythms**- Occurrence of multi-rhythms simultaneously.

- **Call And Response**- The leader makes a statement and there is an answer. This is often found in spirituals and modern day musical selection which utilize solo and chorus.

- **Improvisation**- This technique allows creativity; one has the freedom to makeup as he goes along. This is the main ingredient of jazz and gospel.

Senegal, West African Experience

While visiting Dakar/Senegal, West Africa, I experienced and observed music throughout the day. It was not unusual to awaken to the sounds of drumming, children playing singing games, and an array of sounds imitating music. Individuals could be seen playing instruments, even making them for sale. Throughout the villages, markets and shops music and dance were ever present.

Of course, there are many languages spoken in various parts of Africa. However, in Senegal, the African Republic, former French colony, Wolof is the native language. Musically, the pentatonic scale and scales with intervals of fewer degrees were popular. Some popular instruments observed were the Kora, balafon, xylophone, drums and flutes.

During an evening of entertainment, I visited the clubroom in the hotel. The music consisted of highlife. The music of the band took on various fusions of calypso, tangos, and contemporary popular music. Highlife grew out of the music styles present in the coastal towns of West Africa during the last century, which led to the fusion of indigenous dance rhythms and melodies with influences from the West. One of these sources of outside influences, as stated by John Collins in "Music Makers of West Africa," was from regimental bands associated with the forts and was composed of European musicians. They played military marches, polkas, and popular ballads of the time. Guitar bands and dance bands have been continuously bombarded with foreign musical ideas.

The Goree Island Influence

Many of the Negro spiritual influences may be traced back to West Africa soil. The Goree Island influence, as well as those of other slave trade distribution centers, has contributed great meaning to the spirituals that we hear today. Goree Island is located off the cost of Mainland Africa in Dakar, Senegal. It was a holding place for Africans who were captured and sold to slave traders. Slaves were packed into dungeons before being thrown abroad slave vessels which were bound for the New World America.

The House of Slaves on Goree Island stands, even now, as a reminder of the cruelty and pain that was inflicted upon Africans. On the ground floor of the slave houses or slave quarters were cells designated for women, children, and for men. In some cells slaves were chained to walls. Difficult slaves were also shackled and punished. Still, other cells were no bigger than four feet wide. These were "fattening" rooms for those being strengthened and primed before being sold off. A passage way leads to the infamous "Door of No Return." It was said that Africans who passed through that doorway would never see their homeland again. Outside of the door was the pier where the slave ships docked, and sharks lurked.

Today, many visitors are able to tour Goree Island and the Slave houses. In a trip to the island many of us were torn with emotional stress as we walked through the paths of our ancestors, trying to understand or capture a sense of that tragic history. "We trembled and we cried," the narrator explaining the history, through the interpreter, admonished us not to cry as our ancestors had, but return to America sharing the experience that never again should this happen to our people. The walls are crumbling and worn, but Goree still stands and serves as a memorial and reminder. Today, it is a Senegalese resort which has places to eat, shop, buy souvenirs, and has lovely seaside leisure areas. At the end of the Goree Island guided tour the tourists receive a pilgrimage certificate bearing their African name.

As I walked the paths of our ancestors reflecting upon our heritage, the lyrics of the Negro spirituals became real to me. I envisioned how one would sing songs such as "Jordan's River", "Steal Away", "Sometimes I Feel like a Motherless Child", "O Freedom", "Swing Low", and countless others.

Musical Instruments of Africa

The musical instruments of Africa may be categorized into basic families, similar to those in western musical families. The families are idiophones: self-sounding, sound may be produced without a stretched membrane or vibrating string or reed. Instruments in this family may include shaken idiophones-mbira or sansa (hand piano) and xylophones. These instruments may be categorized as percussion. The membranophone family consists of drums with parchment heads. They range from simple makeshift ones to complex constructed instruments. Drums are usually carved out of solid wood logs and may vary in shape and size. The aerophones, comparable to the western woodwind family, consist of flutes (some made of bamboo, horn tips or gourds, metal tubing and the like. The horns and trumpets make widespread use of animal horns and elephant tusks as trumpets, gourds or bamboo. The trumpets may also be carved out of wood in some societies. The Chordophones (stringed instruments) consist of the musical bow, mouth bow (bow resonated in the mouth), zither, lutes, harps, and lyres).

African Drumming

The beat is the pulse of Africa. Africa and African Americans incorporate rhythms and movement not only on instruments, but through body percussion as well. Rhythmic accompaniment is ever present in musical activities in Africa. There are many types of drums throughout the African continent. Drums can be made from wood and other materials available to them. They may vary in size, shape, and pitch. Africans make musical instruments from the materials and natural resources that they find around them.

Drumming has been used to send messages and codes from one village to another, for ceremonial, leisure activities, and many other occasions. The drum is a symbol of power in many African tribes. Drummers have high status. The position of Master Drummer is inherited. "Sons of Master drummers are taught skills at an early age and spend their entire lives perfecting the art," states Michael Olatunji in <u>Musical Instruments of Africa</u>. Talking drums are very prevalent in Africa. They are used as telephones and telegraphs. All types of messages are sent to announce a birth, death, marriage, events, and sometimes jokes and gossip.

II. SPIRITUAL MOVEMENT

Origin and Development

The Origin and development of the spirituals, stemming from Africans brought to America, are great creations of musical instincts and talents. These songs are handed down from generation to generation via oral tradition. In various studies of the spirituals, it was determined that the earlier ones were built upon the form so common to African songs known as call and response.

The Spirituals

The majority of the spirituals that we know today are those stemming from slavery as Blacks reached the shores of America. However, it has been established that this was, by no means, the beginning of this music, which expressed the Black man's total crucial experiences. Here we still mention that Blacks were torn from their families and loved ones, put an auction blocks, and sold to work as unpaid laborers. Their hopes and aspirations for a better life were very dim, for they were being stripped of their dignity, culture, and freedom. The slaves believed that their only hope for freedom, peace, and contentment was to "cross the River of Jordan", which, to them meant "death". (see figure 1 on pages 28-36)

Freedom from the cruelty and hardships meant to "cross over and be with my Lord". The author visited Jerusalem (Holy Land), Israel to view the Jordan and other biblical places.

"The messages in many of the gospel songs are Biblical in nature. During a visit to Jerusalem (Holy Land), Israel, I had the opportunity to tour many of holy places which are mentioned in the Bible and gospel songs. Some of these sites which included the entire Golgotha's Hill (Calvary Hill where Christ was crucified), Bethlehem, the birthplace of Jesus, The Manger, River of Jordan, Galilee, Jericho, numerous Temples, Mount of Olives and other mountains, Garden of Gethsemane, the Upper Room, the place where Jesus wept, and numerous others. This crusade provided many spiritual and Biblical connections. The experience was one never to be forgotten. It was like a journey through the living Bible.

Music played a very important part in the lives of the Africans, and it was natural for Negroes, as they were often called, to continue their singing after reaching America. One can assume that the pain and sorrow that they bore during enslavement motivated them to sing. These expressions were the spontaneous outpourings of the soul.

Initially, slaves were forbidden to have religious services, for it was felt that they would gain an insight on the morals of life which would not justify their reasons for being enslaved. As time went on, slaves were encouraged to hold religious worship. It was used, however, more as a pacifier.

There is quite a recorded history of Negro spirituals in America. Many prominent musicians and arrangers have performed and penned them to be shared with the world.

Some of these personalities (and this does not include all of them) who contributed to spirituals are Marion Anderson, Nathaniel Dett, Harry T. Burleigh, Paul Robeson, J. Rosamond Johnson, William Dawson, Wendell Whalum, John Work, and many others.

Basically, from slavery, the Negro spirituals were considered as sorrow songs from those who were weary at heart and walked in darkness. The spiritual was often said to be the utterance of individual Negroes about their current experiences.

There are many views of spirituals; however, the summary is simply that spirituals are the emotional expressions of Negro individuals about their particular experience. An example of an emotional spiritual is "Sometimes I Feel like a Motherless Child" (see figure 2).

Spirituals also tell of biblical incidents, for example, "Joshua Fought the Battle of Jericho" (see figure 3).

Others views on the true meaning of spirituals are as follows:

Dr. Melville Charlton, organist for many years at the Union Theological Seminary in New York:

> In a specific sense, it is an American Negro religious folk song.

J. Rosamond Johnson who studied, composed, and sang Black music:

It is an American Negro folk-song, whose rhythm is derived from the African tom-tom beat, with substance of its text based on prayer and religious fervor, set to the characteristics musical cadence of Negro melody.

James Weldon Johnson, brother of J. Rosamond Johnson, known for writing the preface to his brother's collection of spirituals, "The Book of American Negro Spirituals":

They are religious folk songs originated by the Negro in the South and used strictly for purposed of religious worship.

Harry T. Burleigh, composer and soloist at St. George's Church, New York:

The plantation songs known as spirituals are the spontaneous outpouring of intense religious fervor and have their origin chiefly in camp meetings, revivals and other religious exercises. They were never composed, but sprang into life readymade from the white heat of religious fervor.

Many of the spirituals as we know them today have been arranged for trained singers voices. Today, schools, colleges, and universities are singing the scholarly arrangements by such prominent spiritual personalities. (See Appendix for suggested Choral Arrangements). There are many types of spirituals. Some spirituals are narrative, such as "Deep River". Some tell of biblical incidents such as "Joshua Fought the Battle", and many diverse choral arrangements.

At the elementary school level simple spiritual melodies occur in selected materials. High schools, colleges, and universities often include a vast number of spiritual choral arrangements as a part of their repertoire. Churches and other performing groups also enjoy the spirituals. The preservation of this great body of music is vital to our society and should be exposed to generations to come.

Research is continuously being done on the presentation of the Negro Spiritual. Dr. Rosalyn P. Reed-Walker, prominent music educator wrote her doctoral dissertation on "Preserving the Negro Spiritual." She alluded to the fact that many congregations and individuals are very actively engaged in preserving this great body of work known as the Negro Spirituals.

The following are some spirituals that follow the simple call and response structure.

"Swing Low"

Leader	Swing low, sweet chariot,
Congregation	Coming for to carry me home,
Leader	Swing low, sweet chariot,
Congregation	Coming for to carry me home.
Leader	I looked over Jordan and what did I see,
Congregation	Coming for to carry me home?
Leader	A band of angels coming after me,
Congregation	Coming for to carry me home.
	(See figure 8)

There are a number of songs wherein the chorus becomes the most important part, dominating the whole song a coming first, for example, "Steal Away". In this song, the congregation begins with the chorus, singing it in part harmony (See figure 4).

"Steal Away"

Chorus sings: "Steal away, steal away, steal away to Jesus", etc.
Leader comes in with the verse: My Lord, He calls me", etc.
Then the response, in part harmony: "I ain't got long to stay here".
This developed form is carried further in other songs, "Go down, Moses".
Chorus: "go down, Moses", etc.
Leader comes in on verse: "thus saith
the Lord". Etc. (Figure 5).

In a few of the songs, this development is carried to a point where the form becomes almost purely choral. An example of this more complex structure is "Deep River" (See figure 1).

Selected Call and Response Spirituals

The lead and response chant, which is often referred to as the "call and response" idiom, is frequently found in gospel renditions. This form can be traced far back into history. This "call and response" song form, which is of African origin, is present throughout the American Negro's repertoire. One can find many interesting songs that employ the leader-and-chorus type arrangement (See figure 5, 6, and 8)

Dialect

Negro dialect, in its present form, has been used in the United States for the past two centuries. In the South, most white people understand the dialect without any difficulty. The English spoken by the whites does not differ, in some respects, from the dialect, (so great has been the influence of this soft, indolent speech of the Negro). However, Negro dialect may present some difficulties to white people who have never lived in the South, when they attempt to reproduce it in speech or to sing the spirituals. Most of them lose their charm when they are sung in straight English.

Example (Dialect): "I Ain't Gonna Study War No Mo"
Correct English: "I Am Not Going to Study War Anymore"

"Wade in the Water"

Example (Dialect): "Gaud's Go'nuh Trouble Duh Watuh"
Correct English: "God Is Going to Trouble the Water"
Chorus: Wade in duh watuh

Wade in duh watuh childrin
Wade in duh watuh
Gaud's go'nah trouble duh watuh.

If-a you don't believe ah been redeemed,
Gaud's go'nah trouble duh watuh.
Foller me down to Jurdan stream,
Gaud's go'nah trouble duh watuh.

Examples of Dialect Terms

Word or Phrases	Translated Meaning
Ah	oh
An	and
Bet	better
Dat's	that is
Scanlous	scandalous
Sho'nuf	sure enough
Ain't	don't have
Dis	this

Dialect has been a part of the Negro language from slavery through the present time. Many songs, especially spirituals, are recorded in their original language, as mentioned previously. Even the dialect or broken words in gospel music take on a true meaning. Although the English teacher may frown at the grammar, no one can really doubt or criticize the meaning and lessons taught.

A larger number of collections and musical pieces classified as Negro folk songs are Negro spirituals.

Decoding the Spirituals

Spirituals were not only used for religious purposes, but for communication as well. Many signals and messages were sent via "spiritual codes". The slaves were able to decode the messages. Decoding provided alternative or different meanings. In most instances the decoded message implied escape mechanisms. For example, while the spiritual "Wade In The Water" would appear to simply speak of "baptism" to an outsider, the decoded message meant to jump into the water if dogs pursued you in an escape. The reasoning is that dogs cannot pick up the scent in water. There were many other spirituals that the slaves could decode such as, "Follow the Drinking Gourd, Go Down Moses, and Meeting Tonight". (See figure 7)

Preservation

The Negro and his contribution to music during slavery have been handed through the oral tradition through generations. These songs represented their sorrows on this earth, while providing an eternal hope for tomorrow. They provided comfort as they went about their daily tasks.

There are several organizations in existence for the purpose of preserving the Negro Spiritual. One such organization is the "Negro Spiritual Scholarship Foundation." By studying and preserving the Negro Spirituals, much information on the development of slavery can be transmitted. In the United States contemporary composers, arrangers, and vocalists continue performing and keep the heritage alive. Scholars such as Dr. Rosalyn P. Reed-Walker and educator Dan Hodge work to maintain the importance of the Negro Spiritual in both practice and research. Dr. Reed-Walker wrote her doctoral dissertation titled "The Preservation of the Negro Spiritual," and Hodge organized a group of singers in Washington D.C. to perform the Spirituals in their original format. The Negro Spiritual impacted on the evolution of blues, jazz, gospel, and other types of music.

- **Folk Songs of Folk Music** is the spontaneous and traditional music of a people, race, region, or nation. Since folk music is preserved by tradition, the original composer is often unknown. Folk tunes undergo a continual process of change; consequently, there are often many different versions of the same song. Since it is a spontaneous creation, folk music naturally reflects the musical idiom of its people. In form style, folk songs are characteristically simple (see figure 3).

- **The Fisk Jubilee Singers Origin.** They acquainted the masses with spiritual music during their American and European tours from 1871-1878. (See Jubilees).

The following is one of my on-site reflections. I had the opportunity to visit Fisk University on several occasions to participate in individual academic and research projects. There was a feeling of pride within me as I walked on the soil where many of our famous Black scholars and prominent people had matriculated or made other valuable contributions such as graduates William E.B. Dubois, John Hope Franklin, Nikki Giovanni, along with J. Rosamond Johnson, John Work, and the Fisk Jubilee Singers, and many others.

The feeling was overwhelming as I was able to go through the tunnel leading to the center of the campus (circle in front if Jubilee Hall) which was formerly an auction block for slaves. If they were able to escape or seek temporary shelter, they did so via the tunnel. It was at that moment that I felt the real meaning of some of the Negro spirituals.

I also visited the gravesites of several of the pioneer members of the Fisk jubilee singers in Nashville, Tennessee. This experience was provided by Dr. Peter Fields, former Dance Dept. Chair and a prominent member of the Gospel Music Workshop of America, where he teaches dance, Gospel Choreography, Drama and Movement.

Fisk Jubilee "live"

It's the 21st century and the Fisk Jubilee Singers are still carrying on the legacy and tradition for which it started – to travel and introduce spirituals to the masses. Although, the population of the school, Fisk University, changes as students matriculate, graduate and move on, the spirituals are kept alive my prominent, committed academic music professors. This is evidenced by the current Director of the Fisk Jubilee Singers, Dr. Paul T. Kwami. The Fisk Jubilee Singers are "alive and well."

In a recent visit in February, 2014, the Fisk Jubilee Singers, Nashville, Tennesee, were presented in an astounding concert, sponsored by LeMoyne College of Syracuse, New York, and hosted at Bethany Baptist Church, Rev. Phil Turner, Pastor. Dr. Barbara Karper served as Coordinator for LeMoyne College. I had the opportunity to work with the committee. As an African American historian, I am always interested in the music and culture of the genre. In my opinion this allows for the transmittal of history to be passed along to other generations. During the intermission I requested that Dr. Kwami share with some of the choir members the importance of keeping the heritage alive, introduce this historical group and provide comments on the music. This will be an unforgotten experience. He suggested, in summary, that one should know the history, sing it from the heart and soul that the world would see the aesthetics/ beauty, and sing it from a genuine, heavenly work of art.

The audience in attendance was very gratified to engage and witness this outstanding concert by the Fisk Jubilee Singers.

Choral Spiritual Arrangements

Choral and acapela arrangements are continually being performed throughout the world. Scholars are writing and arranging compositions, based on the Negro Spirituals, in collegiate institutions, choral programs, concert halls, churches and other settings. The availability of the music is more prevalent. Some of the arrangements of which to inquire, from past and present sources are collections from Roland Hayes, Roland Carter,

Wendell P. Whalum, Harry T. Burleigh, **Jester Hairston**, Moses Hogan, Evelyn White, William Dawson, Hall Johnson, Andre Thomas, and others. Contemporary writers of all ages are engaging in recording and writing commentary on the heritage. Many gospel writers are presenting their compositions in choral form as well.

Jubilee Songs

Jubilee Songs go back on record to 1896. After Fisk Jubilee's European tours, the singers recorded twenty selections which received critical appraisal in London, Paris, and Berlin. However, the general public never heard very much about the Jubilee. They knew of the spirituals, especially those performed by the great concert artists such as Roland Hayes and others.

The origin of the jubilee song is unique. They come from no musical cultivation whatsoever, but are the simple, ecstatic utterances of wholly untutored minds. The rhythm is often complicated and sometimes strikingly original, with a rare occurrence of triple time, or a three-part measure among them. The reason for this is doubtless to be found in the patting of the feet and the swaying of the body, which are such frequent accompaniments of the singing.

Dr. Philip E. Autry, D.M.A. and Associate Professor and Chair Fisk University Music Department, reflects on Fisk University in the 21st century.

> "In the early twenty-first century, the Fisk Jubilee Singers, under the direction of Paul T. Kwami, continue to keep an active performance schedule throughout the academic year. In the summer of 2007 they travelled to the Republic of Ghana for that country's Jubilee celebration. The visit to the 600-year-old slave prison, Elmina Castle, in Cape Coast, Ghana, was documented in the CD/DVD *Sacred Journey: The Fisk Jubilee Singers* (Nashville: Sunrise Music Group, 2007). The CD *In Bright Mansions* (Nashville: Curb Records, 2003) won a Dove Award from the Gospel Music Association for Best Performance of a Traditional Song. In November 2008, the ensemble was presented with the National Medal of Arts by President George W. Bush."

Spirituals and Gospel Music in the Civil Rights/Peace Movement

In the 20th Century, most Civil Rights issues in the U.S. have been concerned with the rights of Negroes. In 1954, the Supreme Court ruled that segregation in public schools was unconstitutional. Since that time, numerous court decisions have promoted racial integration in various public facilities.

Music has always played an important role in the lives of the Black man. Even from slavery, Blacks sang. A song lifted the heavy burdens as they worked and went along in their struggle for survival. So, even in the struggle for Civil Rights and Peace, singing was an important activity.

"How Did You Feel"

Chorus   Oh, tell me how did you feel when you

Come out the wilderness,
come out the wilderness,

Come out the wilderness?

Oh, tell me how did you feel when you

Come out to the wilderness

Leaning on the Lord.

Verse   Oh, will you fight for freedom

When you come out the wilderness, etc.

"Woke Up This Morning"

Chorus   Woke up this morning with my mind

Stayed on freedom (Oh, well I)

Woke up this morning with my mind

Stayed on freedom

Woke up this morning with my mind

Stayed on freedom-

Hallelu, (Hallelujah),

Hallelujah, (Hallelujah),

Hallelujah

Verse   Walking and talking with my mind, etc.

Spiritual and gospel music had a great effect on the Peace and Civil Rights Movement. The great leaders, Dr. Martin Luther King, Jr., Rev. Ralph D. Abernathy, Rev. Jesse Jackson, Dr. Walter Fauntroy, and others who were very active in the struggle for equality and freedom, were very religious people. In the 20th century, most Civil Rights issues in the U.S. had been concerned with the rights of Negroes. In 1954, the Supreme Court ruled that segregation in public schools was unconstitutional. Since that time, numerous court decisions have promoted racial integration in public facilities. Music has always played an important role in the lives of the Black man. Even from slavery, Blacks sang. A song seemed to lift their heavy burdens as they worked and went along in their struggle for survival. So, even in the struggle for Civil Rights and Peace, singing was an important activity. The majority of the Movement's freedom and protest songs were taken from gospel songs such as, "If You Miss Me From The Back of the Bus" ("If You Miss Me From Praying Down Here"), "This Little Light of Mine" (the freedom song says, "This Little Light Of Freedom, "Free At Last" and others. "Free At Last" is inscribed on the tombstone of the late Civil Rights

Leader, Dr. Martin Luther King, Jr. In fighting for integration, there were all types of protests, such as sit-ins and wade-ins (integration of the swimming pools). In some of the wade-in demonstrations, the protestors sang the old spiritual "Wade In The Water".

The Freedom songs gained a great deal of popularity during the 1960's. Singing has been very important to the movement because people sang at demonstrations, mass meetings, and in jail cells. Singing was used to bring the people together. Many freedom songs evolved s a result of the "March on Washington" in 1963, where the famous "I Have A Dream speech emanated.

The anthem of the Civil Rights movement, "We Shall Overcome), was originally "I'll Be Alright", and it came out of the Negro Church. It began to evolve as a "freedom song" as early as 1945, during the strike of the Food and Tobacco Workers in Charleston, South Carolina.

The following are some of the lyrics that were used in the protest movement. The songs expressed there determination for freedom in all aspects of life, and that there would be "No Turning Back" until they had accomplished their goals.

"Oh Freedom"

Chorus   O' Freedom, O' Freedom,

                O' Freedom over me,

                And before I'd be a slave

                I'll be buried in my grave,

                And go home to my Lord and be free.

Verse   No more moaning…

"Back of the Bus"

Verse   If you miss me from the back of the bus,

And you can't find me nowhere,

Come on up to the front of the bus,

And I'll be riding up there.

Chorus   I'll be riding up there

I'll be riding up there

Just come on up to the front of the bus

I'll be riding up there.

"This Little Light of Mine"

Chorus   This little light of mine- I'm
gonna let it shine-

Oh, this little light of mine- I'm
gonna let it shine-

This little light of mine- I'm
gonna let it shine-

Let it shine, let it shine, let it shine

Verse 1   We've got the light of freedom-

We're gonna let it shine…

Verse 2   Everywhere I go, I'm gonna let it shine…

"We'll Never Turn Back"

Verse 1   We've been buked and
we've been scorned.

We've been talked about
sure's you're born.

Chorus   But we'll never turn back, no,
we'll never turn back.

Until we've all been freed
and we have equality.

Verse 2   We have walked thru the
shadows of death

We've had to walk all by ourselves.

(Chorus)

Verse 3   We have served our time in jail-
With no money for to go our bail-
(Chorus)

Verse 4   We have hung our head and cried
For those like *"lee" who died-
Died for you and died for me-
Died for the cause of equality.
(Chorus)

*(Jimmy Lee Jackson was brutally
murdered during the Civil Rights Era.)*

From Selma to Montgomery

I took a bus ride from Atlanta, Georgia through Montgomery, Alabama. This was the famous route of the Civil Right boycott movement spearheaded by the late Dr. Martin Luther King, Jr. I could hardly imagine the stress, toil and misery as they walked on unknown territory. I rode where they walked. As I was uncomfortable in merely riding the bus, I had pensive thoughts on what the Civil Rights protesters endured. I applaud the courage and the strength that those great leaders faced. Civil Rights members led this march from Selma to Montgomery to advocate voter's rights, though their actual goal had a much broader scope.

FIGURE 1: DEEP RIVER

Deep River

Sometimes I feel like a Motherless Child

Negro Spiritual
Arranged by
H. T. BURLEIGH

Sometimes I feel like a Motherless Child

FIGURE 2 (continued)

FIGURE 2 (continued)

FIGURE 3:

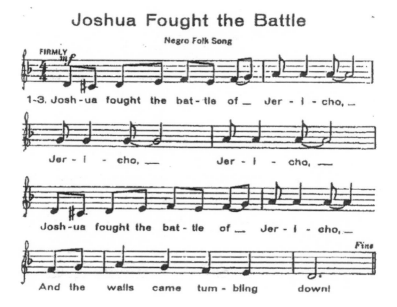

Joshua Fought the Battle

FIGURE 4:

Steal Away

Steal Away

FIGURE 5:

Go Down, Moses

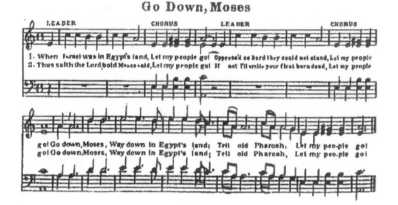

Go Down, Moses

FIGURE 6:
CERTAINLY, LORD

Verse 2.	Well, have you been baptized, etc.
Verse 3.	Well, have you been redeemed, etc.

Certainly Lord

FIGURE 7:
WADE IN THE WATER

Wade in the Water

Swing Low, Sweet Chariot

Swing Low, Sweet Chariot

III. BLACK CONGREGATIONAL SINGING

Singing has always been a powerful source of communication. It is one of the musical components that seems to connect individuals through expression. People of all races and cultures often use a form of music for social and spiritual purposes.

The uniqueness of the Black congregational songs, which are found in many churches are quite overpowering. These congregational songs seem to embrace all of those who are caught up in the participatory experience. One may observe activity from individuals as they react to the various spiritual vibes, such as clapping, nodding, or moving to the beat. These congregational songs may include improvised hymns, spirituals (old and new styles), prayer band singing, praise and worship, gospel songs, and others. This is not to say that other types of music do not exist in the total Black church worship service.

Black congregational song styles have been in existence since the establishment of the Black Church. Many biblical scholars of the church refer to the scripture (Colossians 3:16) that admonishes us to sing psalms, hymns, and spiritual songs.

Devotional Singing

The devotional singing in many Black church congregations is often incorporated to mark the beginning of each service. This is often referred to as the preparation period before what is to follow, whether it is a sermon or other worship activity. It allows the audience time to reflect and "get warmed up". It is a time for testimonies, prayers, and singing. The praise and worship movement has recently become very popular.

A song leader or devotional leader may take charge of this part of the devotional service. There is much audience participation. The audience blends their voices together in rhythm, melody, and harmony to give the utmost praise to the Lord. As the spirit gives utterances of joy, a kind of free-style, improvised rendition evolves, which cannot be adequately penned to music. Many times the accompanist follows along as different song leaders begin to sing. Persons may be more familiar with hymns, regular spirituals, and gospel rather than some of the prayer band repertoire

- **Prayer Band Singing** was described by a member, and mother of the church, New Southern Rock Baptist Church, Washington, D. C., where I served as Minister of Music, Mother Ophelia Williams. She was an advocate for preserving the heritage of Prayer Band Singing. She died at the age of 92. She would say, "These songs are not set to music, they just pop up from the heart, and we sing them. One might sing a line over here, and the spirit catch on, and another get up and sing a line over there." A prayer band union was formed where the singers often traveled on a monthly basis from one town to another, singing and praying all night, taking a break in between. I had the privilege of taking

the Prayer Band to the Smithsonian Institute
in Washington, D. C. to join with Dr. Bernice
Reagan Johnson in a presentation on this music.
Dr. Johnson presented a Prayer Band from an
area, and the two groups educated the public on
this music.

- **Lining Out** was the process by which a lea der
  would give each line of the song and congregation would follow. Sometimes these lines are in a
  singing tone. The congregation being led by the
  persons raising/lining the hymn seemed to follow
  the melodic and harmonic structure. These songs
  often led them into an emotional frenzy, with
  shouting, moaning, running, and giving expressions as the spirit dictated. These songs were not
  penned to music. However, interested musicians
  are studying this style and attempting to notate
  them in order for it to remain in the pages of
  musical history and not become one of the dying
  art forms.

- **Metered Hymns** were often sung by prayer band
  members and still exist in some congregations.
  These songs were often tuned to the old Dr. Isaac
  Watts songs. The most common metered hymns
  were long, common, and short meters. Each of
  these took on a unique metrical sound. These
  songs were handed down from various generations and may vary according to geographical loca-
  tions. No matter what, these songs blended and
  audiences had no problem joining in the singing.

- **Praise and Worship Songs** are becoming ever
  popular among congregations. Often there are

praise teams and dance teams joining in the worship experience. The Praise team serves as leaders in the song services by motivating, lifting hands, and urging free spirit praise and worship among the congregations. The tempo of the song is not the determining factor. Thomas Sinfield in his extensive article on "The Difference Between Praise and Worship." (http//eziearticles.com) commented on this phenomenon. " Praise and worship songs may be fast or slow. Praise and worship as defined is to give thanks and show reverence to the giver of the praise-The Creator." Praise and worship is a relationship with the Deity in many aspects of life and is used in religious services to usher in the spirit. There are scriptural references in the bible for praise and worship, such as "Giving Thanks-Hebrews 13:15", "Dance with The Spirit of David-2 Chronicles 15:12-14." Shirley Caesar, prominent gospel artist, mentions Hebrew words to describe and define praise. Some of these terms are the following:

-Hallal-to laud, boast-Yadah-to worship with extended hands

-Barak-to bless, to declare God reigns

-Tehillah-to sing or laud

-Todah-to extend hands

-Shabach-to command or address in a loud tone

-Zamar-to pluck the strings of an instrument

Finally, Dr. Joan Hillsman states that praise and worship takes the attention from the personal individual and places it on the Lord. Songs will be sung unto Him and not internalized by the performer's unique experiences, relevant to his or her daily situation. Please refer to Praise and Worship songs entitled "I Love You, Lord" and "The Praise and Worship Song."

- **Sacred Harp Singing** stems from singing schools in the colonial period. Its preserved in the South and is also called fasola or shape-note singing. The singing is not accompanied by harp.

IV. GOSPEL MOVEMENT

Toward a Definition of Gospel Music

Gospel is a generic term which takes into account a particular style of performance (vocal and instrumental), purity in values message, as well as delivery. Therefore, when attempting to define, one must be aware of the intent and content of the music.

Immediately when one hears the term "gospel", the mind perhaps, reflects on religious music, the four gospels in the Bible, or one might simply say, "It's church music".

Some authorities say that gospel music is a fusion of Afro-American forms (see Gospel Fusions) such as blues, jazz, spirituals, rock and ragtime. This simply means that the characteristics that are found in these various types are embedded in the music called gospel.

Gospel music is also referred to as the "good news" music. All of these definitions are true. However, gospel music extends far beyond the aforementioned elements. It is a "style" of music that makes use of the African characteristics.

43

A Historical Overview of Gospel Music

Gospel Music has come a long way. It is being arranged, composed, performed, studied and researched by lay persons, scholars, historians, music enthusiasts, and others from all age groups, creeds and nationalities. In other words, gospel music is main stream. It is being presented extensively to music enthusiasts and has transcended almost all ethnic boundaries. The "presentation" of gospel music in the classroom is a key factor, as indicated in this book. This music has influenced other music of the world and helped to shape our society. Even classical composers used Negro thematic materials in their compositions and larger symphonic works, one example is Dvorak's New World Symphony which has the spiritual called "Going Home." Many others may be cited. Gospel groups, soloist and fledgling artists are keeping this art form alive and out front by their contributions to this genre of music.

But, just what is this music? Many scholars will allude to the fact that getting toward a true definition of gospel may be somewhat difficult. However, we must keep in mind the original focus and meaning, that gospel refers to the Biblical reference from the four gospels: Matthew, Mark, Luke and John. Many will say that gospel is the "good news" of the coming of Christ, other will say that it is a religious style, and the conversation goes on and on, for it encompasses all of the above. Gospel music and all of the other African American music forms (music of African decent such as blues, jazz, rhythm and blues, ragtime, spirituals, not forgetting the fusions of rap, go-go, hip-hop elements and other sub-genres), has its roots in Africa. At some time or another, one will hear these element s embedded in gospel music. African characteristics such as call and response, syncopation, cross rhythms, and of course improvisation, (the main ingredient of gospel and jazz), will permeate all African American music.

The History of Black Gospel Music recognizes Thomas A. Dorsey 1899-1993, born in Villa Rica, Georgia, as "The Father of Gospel." Dorsey was a blues pianist for Ma Rainey and Bessie Smith. He was called "Georgia Tom." He was influenced by the hymn writer, Charles A. Tindley. It was stated that Dorsey watched and admired the manner in which Tindley could move the audience with the hymns and wanted to do the same. Many churches denied his entry into the churches, for they stated that he was "stompin' those hymns," so to speak. What he did became a viable component of gospel music (improvised hymns, swaying, clapping, moving, adding highly rhythmical elements).

Dorsey planted the gospel seed for others to follow and spread the gospel around the country and around the world, like Mahalia Jackson, Clara Ward and James Cleveland (1931-1999) to name a few. In 1968, "Oh Happy Day" by Edwin Hawkins bridged the gap from traditional to contemporary gospel. To get a breakdown of the gospel trends and artist by the decade, see the *Historical Time-line. (pages 46-47)*

Included in this book are three Gospel songs that maybe arranged for traditional or contemporary styles:

Songs: We've Come This Far By Faith (Arranged by Dr. Joan Hillsman)
 Glory, Glory Hallelujah (Traditional)
 I Love You, Lord (Dr. Joan Hillsman)

I Love You, Lord

Slow with Feeling
Modulate as desired

Dr. Joan Hillsman

Additional lyrics:
• I Praise you Lord
• I Lift you Up

WE'VE COME THIS FAR BY FAITH

Arr. by Ronald Harbor
Recorded by Concert
Choir of Washington, D.C
Joan Hillsman, Director

Traditional

Historical – Time-line and Survey of Gospel

The late Dr. Pearl Williams- Jones, former professor of music at the University of the District of Columbia, in her document, *A Brief Historical and Analytical Survey of Afro-American Gospel Music*, gives an account of the historical development of gospel (1930-70) according to the following periods:

- **1900-1930- Pre-Gospel Era:** Sociological changes occurred in the Black community (migration from the South by Blacks in search of greater economic opportunities and freedom).

- **The 30's- The Dorsey Era:** The fulfillment of this ideal was first recognized and formulated into gospel song form by the late Tomas A. Dorsey of Chicago, Illinois, the "Father of Gospel Music".

- **The 40's Expansion and Development:** Gospel ensembles and quartets were organized and began traveling to the East and West to help fill the increasing demands for this new, vitally moving religious music. Commercial concerts were head-lined with Sister Rosetta Tharpe, Sally Martin, Roberta Martin, Mahalia Jackson, and others.

- **The 50's- Gospel Chorus:** Ensembles of two to six voices, commonly referred to as "gospel groups", were prevalent "Clara Ward Singers, Staple Singers, Caravans, Alex Bradford, Davis Sisters and others).

- **The 60's- Gospel Choirs:** Choirs began to flourish (various sizes); Edwin Hawkins' "O Happy Day" marked a turning point. Personalities: Clinton

Uttterback, Jesse Dixon, Mattie Moss Clark and
Myrna Summers of D.C. ("God Gave Me a Song").

- **The 70's and 80's Gospel Music Expansion:**
  During the 70's and 80's, gospel music continued
  to progress and expand. This was the era for the
  formation of large choirs such as Charles Fold
  Singers and James Cleveland's California Chorus.
  The 70's also continued to see the flowering of
  Andrae' Crouch, the late Danibelle Hall and The
  Hawkins, to name a few. During the 80's, some of
  our leading quartets such as the Mighty Clouds
  of Joy, Gospel Keynotes, Williams Brothers, and
  Jackson Southernaires excelled. The Winans and
  Hawkins Family flourished. Out of the Hawkins
  Family came their individual family members as
  solo artists such as Tramaine Hawkins and others.

- **The 90's, 21st Century, and beyond:** During this
  period, we are experiencing a renaissance of
  ideas from more contemporary and progressive
  gospel artists. Gospel is being mainstreamed and
  incorporated in places where previously denied.
  Such venues are educational and curricula settings, Catholic services, Broadway, cathedrals
  and international areas to name a few. Advanced
  technology has greatly impacted the field of
  gospel. Gospel is on the world-wide web. More
  scholars are viewing gospel music as a career. The
  future of Gospel music, due to the impact of technology, will perhaps allow its ability to connect
  to college music departments, the music industry,
  announcer's guilds, Broadway, plays, and drama,
  and the online market in a global perspective.

The Progress of Gospel Music

Gospel music has made tremendous progress, whereas it is being performed in many places where it was previously denied (educational curriculum, Catholic Churches, and prominent performance areas).

When we look at the progress that gospel music has made within the last decade, we will find that the music is ranked very high among other genres and is held in high esteem among listeners. Gospel has progressed to mainstream venues. Radio, television, commercialism and technology have greatly impacted upon its progress," states Ron Jones, Radio Music Consultant, Louisville Kentucky, Professor at the University of Louisville, Administrative Assistant for the Gospel Music Workshops of America (Announcers Guild), Dean for the Church of God in Christ music department, and travels with the Black Diamond Choir of Louisville, which consists of 65 students singing Black gospel.

Commercially, gospel music merchants attest to the record breaking sales from sheet music and other technology such as records, cassettes, CD's, MP3 downloads, etc. Gospel is on top Billboard and other rating charts. The award shows provide recognition for many gospel artists who excel in their field. Gospel music channels provide exposure to this great body of music. Many gospel artists and record labels are able to survive financially due to the surge and interest in this music. Artists are able to make a professional career in the field of gospel. Some artist sales have reached platinum status. Renowned producers in the recording industry affirm the productivity and growth of Gospel Music in the 21st century. Music technology is on the rise. Gospel musicians are able to utilize some of the same electronic and technological devices to enhance their music. Music computer programs and software is available at churches and other performances, therefore, having the capability of transcription and full orchestration.

Reflecting upon recording artist and their sales, we see that many artists are able to enjoy affluent, lucrative careers in gospel music. "Some have reached platinum status (selling over a million)," states Ron Jones. "Gospel music is real soul music. It speaks to the real nature of Mankind," (Ron Jones), which is the soul.

Gospel music is alive and well. It is ranking highly among the other forms of African American music. There is an increasing demand and quest for more knowledge of gospel music by people of all walks of life (educators, clergymen, lay persons, community leaders, and music enthusiasts). Although gospel music has been in existence since the early 20th century, it has gained popularity and attention due to pioneers like Thomas A. Dorsey, Mahalia Jackson, and others. Gospel is now a reality and powerful influence in our society. It is very popular and is being performed extensively. It is recognized in the commercial industries, institutions of higher learning, prominent organizations, and has high visibility internationally.

Many Catholic churches and schools have included gospel music as part of their programs and services. Some Catholic churches have devoted their entire service to the "Gospel Mass". This brings about another medium for gospel music enhancement. Gospel music adds another innovative dimension to the Catholic service as many parishioners have stated.

Gospel music is integrated into the educational settings: schools, colleges, and universities. As early as elementary school, teachers are beginning to incorporate gospel music into their classroom programs. High schools, colleges, and universities infuse gospel into their programs as well. Many educators matriculated in schools where gospel music was not accepted, and certainly was not included as a viable part of the curriculum. However, gospel is now an instructional trend that must be acknowledged as society moves toward the 21st century. Therefore, many educators are now studying, writing gospel, attending seminars and workshops, and preparing themselves to administer gospel music. (See "Gospel Music in the Educational Setting", chapter six).

As gospel continues to progress, we can observe the flourishing of it in the entertainment arena such as Broadway, and other places. The late professor Alex Bradford, who worked along with others in promoting plays and musicals such as *Don't Bother Me, I Can't Cope, Black Nativity, What's A Friend For, Your Arms Too Short to Box With God,* and more, helped to blaze the dramatic trail- that many artists are now able to tread with ease. Gospel music plays, and other dramas are not rare or viewed as being in an unfamiliar setting. Great gospel giants such as Andrae Crouch, Rev. James Cleveland, Edwin Hawkins, and many others have performed in places such as Carnegie Hall, Mormon Tabernacle (GMWA Performance in 1991), John F. Kennedy Center for the Performing Arts, along with other auditoriums of local, national and international acclaim.

Many organizations often include gospel music as a part of their various events in part or as a whole concert. Gospel music enhances, brings excitement and inspiration to its audiences. Music in general, sets the tone for openings and inclusions in agenda and activities throughout the world.

Some of today's top selling artists are Kirk Franklin, Patty Labelle, J. Moss, Kurt Carr, Tye Tribbett and GA, Donald

Lawrence, Yolanda Adams, Mary Mary, Donnie McClurkin, Marvin Sapp, The Winans, The Clark Sisters, Juanita Bynum, Fred Hammond, Rance Allen, Richard Smallwood, Byron Cage, to name a few. There are many fledging artists from local churches, colleges and other arenas.

(Interview with Ron Jones forthcoming---Will send)

International Connection

Gospel music is very popular around the world. It is enjoyed tremendously as an art form globally. There are many gospel groups in countries such as Germany, Sweden, Bahamas, Japan and others. Festivals and concert tours are held and draw record-breaking crowds to witness the Black gospel sound. Many international groups have connections with artists, musicians and educators. They network and exchange gospel information. The James Cleveland Gospel Music Workshops of America (GMWA) has several international chapters that meet at their annual conventions. Gospel educators are also invited to Europe to conduct workshops and engage in concert performances.

Instruments Used In Gospel

After the decline of slavery, there was the desire for a happier, jubilant, moving type of music. Therefore, gospel music came on the scene. Gospel music, especially contemporary, employs such characteristics as cross-rhythms, call and response, syncopation, and the main ingredient, improvisation. A substantial amount of instrumentation is utilized in gospel music as well, possibly appearing as complex melody, rhythms, or intricate harmony. It is no surprise that gospel musicians, composers, and arrangers would make use of some band and orchestral instruments.

During the earlier years of gospel music's popularity, instruments were sometimes forbidden in the churches for controversial reasons, referring it as secular or worldly in nature. Thomas A. Dorsey, "The Father of Gospel Music", who was a former blues singer and pianist, was not allowed in churches at first because he added the "beat to the hymns", so to speak. In some churches today, there are still restrictions placed on the use of instruments in a worship service. Many gospel musicians will often refer to the 150th Psalm of the Bible which gives permission to "Praise the Lord with the instruments". Some of the instruments in the 150th Psalm can be compared to our modern day instruments.

The earlier style of gospel, referring to the traditional style, made use of very few musical instrumental. The basic instruments were piano, organ and drums, later adding the bass guitar. As times progressed and more diverse arrangements for compositions evolved, there were no limits to the instrumentation used in the music. Today, especially with the availability of technology, gospel artists are utilizing full orchestras, synthesizers, or whatever instruments they desire.

The Gospel Singer and His Technique

Gospel artists sing with confidence. They have a sense of security and well-being. The most critical audience will be won over by the sincere, free delivery of gospel singers.

Many of the gospel songs are arrangements. The singer may express the delivery in a free style which is unrestricted in every way. The singer, when performing many gospel compositions, has the freedom to modify the music to add his unique personal expression. This may not be easily done in presenting choral versions of the spiritual. There are basically three types of spirituals in short, the syncopated, segmented type such as "Little Lamb, Little Lamb", the call and response type "Have You Got Good Religion"; and the long narrative type "Deep River". The gospel singer may sing the song as he feels it, and will utilize much improvisation, repetition, and adlib techniques. Whether it is narrative, call and response, or segmented, it depends on the ability of the singer to interpret, or "worry" the notes. It is sometimes difficult singing the music strictly as written, for the singer gives allegiance to the spirit and emotions in their delivery.

Spotlight on Prominent Gospel Artists

Mahalia Jackson was born in New Orleans in 1911, and died in Chicago in 1972. Her father worked as a stevedore, as a barber after working hours, and as a clergyman on Sundays. Mahalia sang in her father's choir from the age of five. As a child, she heard records of Ida Cox, and Bessie and Mamie Smith, but her interest remained with sacred music rather than blues. After attending school through the eighth grade, she went to Chicago at the age of sixteen, worked as a hotel maid, and packed dates in a factory. She led in a quartet of church singers. She won worldwide fame as the "World's Greatest Gospel Singer".

Professor Thomas A. Dorsey was born in Villa Rica, Georgia in 1899. Dorsey, the great writer of gospel songs, is a pioneer in the gospel field. He is known as the "Father of Gospel". He is to gospel music what W.C. Handy is to the blues. A lot of folks do not know that gospel songs have been compassed and written by Negro musicians like Professor Dorsey. There are more gospel arrangers the composers.

Before Professor Dorsey got saved by the Lord, he was a pianist for Ma Rainey, one of the first blues singers. His nickname was "Georgia Tom". The late Rev. James Cleveland was born in Chicago, Illinois. He had been singing for many years. He has sung for large audiences all over the world, and was known to many as the "King of Gospel" or the "Crown Prince of Gospel."

Rev. James Cleveland was the founder of the Gospel Music Workshop of America, Inc. (GMWA), an organization of over 30,000 members who meet annually across the U.S.A. Founded in 1967; the GMWA is the largest artistic organization of its kind in the world.

There are approximately 185 active chapters of the workshop within the national structure. Several International chapters have organized throughout the GMWA, which includes the United Kingdom, Caribbean, Europe and Asia. Many artists have been promoted and flourished as prominent recording personalities. Rev. Cleveland is to be applauded for his contributions in providing a professional arena for artists to exhibit their talents. The GMWA is a structured organization with many divisions such as the Academic Division, Radio Announcers' Guild, Evangelistic Board, and many others. Personally, I have been active in the GMWA for forty years, serving in many leadership capacities such as: National Scholarship Chairperson (Academic Division), Operations, and most recently elected to the National Board of Directors (2008). Presently, Bishop Albert Jamison is the Chairman of the Board of Directors.

The purpose of the workshop is to improve the standards of gospel music, especially in the churches. Rev. Cleveland was also the pastor of a church in Los Angeles, California. He recorded such hits as "Peace Be Still", "Stood on the Banks", and many others.

Clara Ward was born in Philadelphia, Pennsylvania in 1925, and died January 16, 1973 at the age of forty-eight. Clara Wood was a noted songwriter, singer, director, and musician. Clara had been highly acclaimed at the Newport Jazz and Folk Festivals, the Ravinia Music Festival in Chicago, and the Chevron Hilton Hotel in Sydney, Australia in October of 1967, and was held over to February on 1968. Clara had received rave reviews from all over the world.

Clara Ward recorded for over ten record companies, including Columbia, Savoy, Capitol, Vanguard, and just before her death, United Artists, leaving behind some of her most popular and never to be forgotten music. Clara had been playing the piano since she was eight years old, and singing since the age of five. Some of her favorite songs were: "Redeemed", "Anywhere in Glory", "Surely God Is Able", "Hold Back the Tears", and "How I Got Over."

Clara died in California on January 16, 1973 after suffering a heart attack. Clara was laid to rest as Forest Lawn Memorial Mausoleum. In that same mausoleum, other "greats" such as Gracie Allen, Nat "King" Cole, and Earl Grant also were laid to rest.

We cannot forget the other great pioneers who have brought gospel music to its current position. The list is too numerous to mention here. However, great contributors, past and present, such as the Roberta Martin Singers, the Davis Sisters, Gospel Harmonettes, Dorothy Love Coates, Dorothy

Norwood, Alex Bradford, Harmonizing Four, Pilgrim Jubilees, Soul Stirrers, Dixie Hummingbirds, Brother Joe May, Sallie Martin, and others, should be recognized in this great field.

Contemporary Gospel Artists

While proceeding into the 21st century, as society embarks upon a new wave of technological influences, many areas are being influenced. In music, we see much advancement in the recording industry and the world of music at large. Synthesizers, computers, electronic devices and other modern innovations are contributing to the ever-changing sound of this music. Many younger performing artists are utilizing advanced techniques and skills to direct the attention of the masses toward their music. The contemporary sounds differ from those taught in traditional schools. Early pioneer gospel artists made use of the simple musical elements of harmony and instrumentation. Many contemporary sounds entail many of those elements heard in secular music. The new generation recording artists such as Take Six, The Winans and Family, the Hawkins, Richard Smallwood, Commissioned, and other inspiring gospel artists are incorporating unique musical ideas into their music ministries. Some of their forerunners such as Billy Preston, the late Donny Hathaway, the Mighty Clouds of Joy, Staple Singers, and others were contemporary in their times.

Gospel Music:
A Fusion of Other African American Forms

Gospel music is often said to be a fusion of the other forms such as blues, jazz, ragtime, popular, rhythm and blues. Due to the fact that each of these forms may have distinct characteristics, the basic African musical features over-lap and fuse together, sometimes making it very difficult to separate. Current contemporary gospel may incorporate elements of hip hop, rap, go-go, and other elements which constitute what is know as a fusion- the blending of more than one style. All of these styles have definite influences on gospel music.

Work Songs, Field Hollers, and Cries

- **Work songs** were sung by slaves as they worked in the fields. They were similar to those sung in Africa. After slavery was over, Blacks got other kinds of jobs. Therefore, the Work songs changed somewhat (i.e. "I've Been Working on the Railroad"). Field hollers and cries were also expressions by Blacks in the fields as they worked.

- **Spirituals** were born during slavery. These songs were sung out of emotional fervor pouring from their hearts. Slavery was not a happy time. The conditions were cruel. Blacks were brought from Africa, put on auction blocks, torn from families, loved ones and friends, and sold as slaves to work for unpaid labor.

- **Blues** are often referred to as the secular spiritual. Blues dealt with events on earth just as they were, while the spirituals emphasized heavenly things. The blues are characterized by a particular kind of blues scale and the use of "blue notes" where the sound is slurred on the flatted third and seventh (sometimes fifth and sixth). The blues formula consists of three lines, one line repeated with a third line (punch line) which gets into the development of the song (AAB form). Blues singers often moan, shout and slide from one pitch to another, as the African singer sometimes does. The most common types of blues were 8 bar and 12 bar blues.

- **Rhythm and Blues** is often referred to as a blues with a big beat. As the blues became important to instrumentalists as well as vocalists, the music gradually took on a new character. A repetitious rhythmic beat became a standard accompaniment. The repetition unifies the music. Blues with a "big beat" is now music by groups of professional entertainers, rather than amateur soloists. Important figures in the development: Ray Charles, Fats Domino, Chuck Berry, Hank Ballard, etc.

- **Gospel** music came on the scene after the decline of slavery. Gospel music became popular around 1940. The music is a happy, jubilant of music with much movement, instrumentation, and improvisation. There are several type of gospel music; however, the two most popular are traditional and contemporary. Traditional gospel is simple in melody, rhythm, and harmonic structure (I, IV and V7 whereas contemporary gospel deals with more diversified, instrumentation, etc. Gospel is a religious music with spiritual messages based on Biblical principles. It has a message of "truth".

- **Ragtime** is a piano music which is characterized by the left hand playing a percussive stomping rhythm while the right hand plays an exciting "off beat" melody. Most of the early rag pianists did not read music; the style developed as they played. The music they played was similar to that music slaves had used for dancing on the plantations.

- **Jazz** was the first music that people considered truly "American music". Jazz has its roots in the blues and ragtime. Much jazz is based upon the same kind of scale as the blues. Improvisation is the basic ingredient on most jazz. In jazz, the players may improvise as they play. Jazz is not so much a kind of music as it is a way of performing music. There are many types of jazz.

- **Boogie-Woogie** is a style of piano music based on the blues. The boogie bass line was first called the "walking bass". The boogie bass consisted of left-hand ostinatos of eight notes per measure.

- **Rap** is a Black cultural expression; the words are rhythmically recited, chanted or sung over music. It is a rhymed storytelling style accompanied by highly rhythmic, electronic- based music. It emerged during the 80's and 90's.

- **Hip-Hop is** a 20th century cultural expression which includes rap, communal singing of melodies and lyrics, free style often coupled with technology.

V. THE GRIPPING EFFECT OF GOSPEL

When speaking of the "gripping" effect of gospel, we are thinking in terms of the power and influence that gospel has on the singer's vocal style and delivery. Once gospel music has become a serious part of an individual's experience or culture, it is often quite difficult to sever its ties. Generally speaking, one can usually tell a singer who was originally a gospel performer. Those characteristics seem very pronounced. Gospel has a gripping effect, and it is the foundation of a large percentage of Black performing artists today. It has been said "once a gospel singer, always a gospel singer".

Gospel is gripping; gospel is compelling; gospel is forever. If one listens to it, and practice its teachings, perhaps his life may become richer. It has moral effects. Yes, gospel seems to have that gripping effect. Often it is very easy to detect the gospel flavor or sound in rock and roll, and even pop artists. Somehow, gospel leaves its stain within the human soul. This is very evident in such artists as Aretha Franklin, who was very active in her father's church in Detroit, Michigan. One writer stated that Aretha only changed a few words in her R&B singing. Instead of saying "God", she says "my man". Wilson Pickett and Donny Hathaway, who come from a family of gospel talents, also exhibit that gospel flavor in their compositions. Therefore, we can say that gospel music has an effect on the popular rock and roll singer.

Popular and R&B Artists Transition

As we view R&B and pop artists performing, many of them got their start in the church. The church has served as a training ground for many popular artists. One could always go to the church and be accepted, even when they could not go elsewhere. Some gospel artists have pursued the pop field and vice versa. They are referred to as "cross-over" artists. They were often criticized by the church for making this transition for whatever reason. Rev. Jesse Jackson, Civil Rights leader and Director of Operation PUSH once stated, "I long for the day that the great gospel singers do not have to desert our tradition just to make a living". In many instances, gospel artists have not gained the support as artists in other fields. However, many gospel artists are becoming very successful, not only spiritually, but financially as well. One so-called "cross-over" artist stated that he did not really cross genres but maintained his gospel style and technique in his performances.

Some popular artists who came from the gospel experience are Lou Rawls, Brook Benton, Solomon Burke, Dionne Warwicke, the late Donny Hathaway, Aretha Franklin, Ray Charles, Elvis Presley (sang gospel hymns and other sacred music), Sam Cooke, Dee Dee Warrick, The Staples, Jennifer Holliday, Patti LaBelle, and others.

Many artists do not limit their style to a particular form but use their creativity to include all types of music.

The Church

The church is an organization of religious believers. There are many denominations within the Christian church, such as Baptist, Methodist, Catholic, and others.

Early slaves were looked upon as being inferior. Therefore, Christianity and "The Good Book" was thought to be too good for them. The house slaves adapted white mannerisms, customs, and their religion first. However, the Episcopal Church and the Presbyterian Church did not seem to fit for the slaves. This was due to the social class of the membership. The Methodists and the Baptists, during the 1800's, sent missionaries to the slaves. The Baptists won because of the freedom allowed in the church. It also included the procedure of baptism, which was "total immersion in water".

"Spirit Possession", as it was called in African religions, was also intrinsic to Afro-Christianity: "getting' the spirit", "getting' religion", or "getting happy" were indispensable features for the early American Negro church, and even today of the non-middle class and rural Negro churches.

Music was always an important part of the total emotional configuration of the Negro church. It acted, in most cases, as a catalyst for those worshippers who might suddenly "feel the spirit".

The first Afro- Christian music differed from earlier work songs and non-religious shouts:

1. In subject matter and content; and

2. Religious matter became more melodic and musical. "The spirit will not descend without song".

This is an old African dictum incorporated into Afro-Christian worship. The Negro church has always been a "church of emotion". In Africa, ritual dances and songs were integral parts of African religious practices and have been pretty well documented, although, I would suppose, rarely understood. This heritage of emotional religion was one of the strongest contributions that the African culture made to us Afro-Americans. Slavery served well to give the Black salve as huge reservoir of emotional energy which could be used up in his religion.

Yes, it is true that some churches are very emotional, sometimes mournful, sometimes tense, and moving. Often, when one is moved to pray, he prays out loud. The others hum in harmony and interject their feelings when the Spirit urges. The ceremony throbs throughout with song and rhythm. The preacher half-sings, half-shouts the sermon, while the congregation encourages him with expressions of "Hallelujah", "Praise the Lord", "Oh yes", and "Amen". They want to capture the feeling of the spirit more than the sense of the words.

Gaining strength from a hope of happiness in death, the choir sings out a good old gospel such as "Don't Worry about Me". Finding comfort in the knowledge that Jesus was also persecuted, their voices rise: "Surely He Died on Calvary" or "Were You There When They Crucified My Lord?"

In talking with various ministers about the role that gospel music plays upon their and the church, most of the response were of a similar nature. Some said that gospel music sets a tone or atmosphere for service.

The Rev. Claude Jeter, a prominent singer as well as a minster in New York, states that emotionalism seems to be the "thing" in today's churches and audiences, and in some cases if the singer is not emotional, one would that he didn't sing well. In other word, people are making a "program" or "show" out of the gospel service. The late Rev. James Seigler of Washington D.C., a very dynamic minster, depended to a large extent on his choirs. He loved gospel singing and before the message was delivered, he requested a sermonic selection from the choir in order to set the mood for the spoken word.

The late Rev. James Cleveland, "The Crown Prince of Gospel," stated that the gospel music softens the ears for the sermon. It is as though the gardener were cultivating the soil for the planting of the seeds.

Musicians may find it very difficult to secure a church music job that doesn't involve the gospel choir, even in the most prominent Black churches. "As serious musicians, one has to face that fact," says Lena McLin, retired faculty member of Chicago's Kenwood High School, and an exceptional musician. Congregations and sacred music programs incorporate a variety of music to meet the spiritual needs of all parishioners.

Most of the responses were of a similar nature. All of the ministers applauded the positive effect that gospel music has on the worship services. However, some may have varying opinions on how the music is presented in conjunction with the spoken word. For example, the renowned pastor and recording artist of sermons and services, the late Rev. **Bennett** Smith of Buffalo, New York stated in an interview, that he preferred a hymn before he took his sermon text. He also stated that some ministers prefer the choir singing an up-beat, or so-called "hot" selection before his sermon. Many times the audience may become caught up in the emotionalism of the choir, sometimes causing and the minister to ride on their coat-tail, so to speak. He stated that the message should be able to stand on its own.

Shouting

During antebellum days, shouting was as much a part of the Sunday afternoon service as the sermon. By 1900, however, the more fashionable Negro preachers felt that this mode of worship was not correct, since it did not conform to the conventional pattern of the white man's service. They began to frown upon the religious dance, as they did upon the use of the word "Amen" and similar responses by the congregation. Even so, the hold of shouting is tenacious and is still practiced in some churches today. The word "shouting" was often used in designating the religious ring-dance, which was enjoyed during plantation days after meeting and church service. Formerly, writers thought that the Negro used the word "shouting" because dancing was so sinful that it was wise to avoid even the name. It would not be surprising to see someone break out into a shout or sometimes referred as "the Holy Dance." They often validated this practice from biblical references of praising Him, with a dance, primarily from the Ecclesiastes 3 and along with the book of Samuel where "David danced with all his might." Today, religious chorography, drama, and dancing are incorporated in sacred music programs and services.

Those who have traveled in Africa and have seen native dancing are convinced that the shout of the American Negro is nothing more than a survival of an African tribal dance, and quite as typical of Africa as the dance itself. (Records #6 and #10 of the series made in the Belgian Congo by the

Denis-Roosevelt expedition are strikingly similar). The Negroes substituted words of the Old Testament for those of their native land.

Morals and Values

Gospel music is biblically based in its messages. Gospel music instills moral values in those who are receptive. The messages of truth, hope, and courage can relate to life long experiences.

There are a vast number of people who believe in the deity and religious power. Many were very much concerned about the Supreme Court's decision of "Prayer In The Schools", that children should not pray in school. The late gospel promoter, Mancel "Speedy" Warrick, (father of Dee-Dee and Dionne Warwick), launched a letter writing campaign in the early 70's. Petitions, (along with a recording by the Hillsman Singer's "Please Let Us Pray In School"), for the restoration of prayer in the schools were sent to governmental agencies, senators and other dignitaries and legislators. The message touched some of the consciousness in support of the effort. This led to the "Pray in School" March on the White House. Several responses were received, for they heard the powerful message on the recording that had spread over the airwaves. The music captured the attention of the listeners.

The elements of gospel music, rhythm, melody, harmony, and form are unique in characteristics. However, the message conveyed can have an impact and lasting effect on ones life. There are many powerful lyrics that evoke positive thoughts such as: Build Your Hopes on Things Eternal, Never Let Go of His Hand, Wise Man-Foolish Man, Keep on Believing, and others. These messages are not restricted to religious beliefs alone, but can be analyzed and equated to life in general. There are no age limits to the teaching of morals and values. From elementary, secondary, college and adult levels, many individuals can relate to the morrows of the message.

VI. A YOUTHFUL PERSPECTIVE: GOSPEL IN THE NEW MILLENIUM

With contributions by Rickey Payton, Sr.

Rickey Payton, Sr. is in charge of a prominent youth group in Washington, D. C., called The Urban Nation H.I.P.H.O.P. choir. He presents a detailed, thorough account of traditional and contemporary, as it is perceived by youth in the area. He states the following:

"Gospel Music is a unique style religious songs born out of the African American experience. It Carries message of good news, hope, inspiration, joy, and the love of God. The sound of gospel music has changed over the years with many influences from various genres. These styles include blues, ragtime, jazz, calypso, R&B, contemporary, soul, rock, and hip-hop and rap amongst many others. The influence of all of these genres has diluted the true original art form of traditional gospel music into a more complex and versatile style. Though mixed with all of these distinct forms, the fact still remains that traditional gospel is the foundation that all of these art forms are built upon. It will always be around and alive forever.

Looking at gospel music from a youth perspective and bridging the gap in teaching them about the traditional versus contemporary is a recurring struggle. We must look for more innovative ways to engage our youth when much of what they see, hear, and are exposed to is built around pop culture. I run a youth choir in Washington D.C. called The Urban Nation H.I.P. H.O.P. Choir. Focusing on the acronym H.I.P. H.O.P. (Hope, Integrity, Power - Helping Our People), the choir's mission is to channel the creative and artistic energies of a targeted group of youth into a dynamic structured group that will foster excellence in all facets of their lives. They gain a better understanding and awareness of their heritage by performing a variety of musical styles. In doing this, I like for them to be exposed to various styles of music and making a connection. When talking to a former member of Urban Nation, Katrina Bello, I asked her take on traditional gospel versus contemporary music. She responded and said, "Traditional gospel music evokes a deeper feeling for me as opposed to contemporary. Though, I love contemporary gospel and can take a message away from it, its more about tapping my foot and bobbing my head and just does not evoke the same type of emotion in me."

The Hip-Hop Movement in Gospel

Hip-Hop and Rap Music was developed out of a need to bring about a more socially conscious awareness of the black experience in America. It also gave a platform to address various strong and personal issues in the black community, with a strong emphasis on rhythm and heavy bass. This music arose from the mixing of Jamaican and American musical cultures. Though highly controversial, it triggered a strong connection and level of emotion via the youth. Commonly perceived in a negative light, there are artists in the hip-hop world who use it for a positive influence. In keeping it real, the reality is since the influence of hip-hop is a drawing power amongst our youth, it poses the question, "Why not use hip hop to connect them to gospel music?" The reason that they connect is because it is exciting for them, gives them a platform, and addresses a lot of their issues. Such artists who have done this effectively in the hip-hop and rap genre of gospel to mention a few include Tonex, Kirk Franklin, Tye Tribbett, Jay Moss, Toby Mac, Kiki Sheard, MaryMary, Israel and New Breed. They serve as fine examples of artists who have blended the music of hip-hop and gospel and kept the message the same. As a result, you will find more young people involved in church and community choirs, therefore connecting them to the many styles of music, including traditional gospel.

I think that both traditional and contemporary gospel music have their places respectively. The future of gospel music is on the rise and is now accepted and can be heard on radios, television, videos, movies, universities and around the world. Over the years, the blending of musical idioms has become very popular. They are all art forms and are connected, and rooted in deep, complex history of African Americans. I feel that as long as we remain true to the foundation of gospel music, we can always be creative and build upon it.

Student Surveys on Campuses

A random survey was taken among selected youth in Washington D.C. Metropolitan area and other states. The surveys intent was to determine the types of music that is most appealing to them, along with other thoughts on gospel and youth in general. Surprisingly to say, surveys revealed that not all youth are hooked on upbeat, loud-sounding, secular type elements that often occur in contemporary gospel arrangements. There were youth that stated that they enjoyed traditional gospel, and that they thought that rap and other new fad secular idioms maybe should not infiltrate the worship service. One youth said, "Let church be church". A large number of youth, however, preferred contemporary elements of gospel. There are several testimonies given by students such as Chania Dillard, Michelle Brooks, Kennan Dupree, Donna Smith, and Melody Johnson. These were students who sang under my direction in Bowie State University's gospel choir in Bowie, Maryland. All of their testimonies were based on the fact that their choir experiences and campus ministries contributed to their spiritual lives and enhanced their moral standards through their participation of activities in the choir. Many of them have since pursued their own careers in various fields but stay in contact with me, grateful for contributing to their spiritual esteem through gospel music. Gospel was a vehicle for which they obtained discipline, professionalism, self-respect, and positive enrichment. The current director of the Bowie State gospel choir, Prof. Latonya Wrenn, upholds those standards inherited from the previous program. The program receives one academic course credit, has recorded CDs and participates in the Gospel Music Workshop of America (GMWA). There is a need for youth to understand the history of gospel, pioneers, and all styles (including spirituals, congregational sings, hymns, etc.) in order that they may be well-rounded. Thereby, being able to appreciate all kinds of music and becoming musically literate. This music must continue to be handed down from generation to generation. This oral tradition must not die. Opportunities through seminars, workshops, and educational settings are very crucial to preserving the heritage of music as a people.

In Syracuse, New York, musicians are actively engaged in large venues such as festivals, the annual New York State Fair and other community choirs. Youth come together in mass choirs to share the experience in gospel music. The popularity of these gatherings exuberates the youth as much as their audiences.

The educational systems are making progress in incorporating gospel and other African American forms into the curriculum. (See Gospel in the Curriculum)

Youth in Gospel

Young people have a renewed interest in gospel music. Gospel has touched the lives of youngsters of all ages in homes, schools, and universities. A large number of youth purchase the music of their choice. Today, there are more types from which to choose, due to the fact that many artists are recording diversified music in a progressive and contemporary idiom which appeals to their audience. Youth are relating to the music of urban gospel artists. This generation of youth are looking for different styles of music that would incorporate their experiences of today, such as hip hop, rap, and other styles. Maestro, as he is called, Ricky Payton formed the popular Urban Nation Hip Hop Choir in Washington, DC. He states that in some instances, the new generation of youth are looking for something different to which they can relate. Although he uses elements of hip hop, movement, and jubilation in his music, he does not fail to teach the traditional background of gospel; on which the shoulders this music stands.

This contributing article on traditional vs. contemporary gospel music is being shared by Maestro, Rickey Payton, Sr. He has worked with youth over the years as a part of the Urban Nation H.I.P. H.O.P. Choir of Washington, DC. He is a voting member of the Grammy Awards, and a prolific composer, producer and teacher of music.

VII. GOSPEL MUSIC: A PART OF THE CURRICULUM

If we are to begin exposing the various cultures to a cross-section of music, the classroom is a good place to start. Gospel music should not be excluded. There have been many concerns regarding gospel music in the curriculum. The concerns range from questioning its quality, importance, content delivery, and infringement. Perhaps, this tip will help. As far as quality and vocal production, do not sacrifice the level of excellence. Proper vocal techniques when performing or practicing, the music is essential. As for infringements, teach the elements of gospel not the doctrine (See Teaching the Content of Gospel).

When incorporating the various styles of music, the instructor, first, has the responsibility for understanding the style, history and performance practices of the music. Students should be exposed to all types of music. Gospel, as well as other African American music forms, belong in the curriculum at all levels from elementary through higher learning. If it is not incorporated within the pre-college music studies, we run the risk of other cultures not understanding this great body of materials. Likewise, the African American student, for lack of experience and knowledge, may miss a potential career opportunity. This section will give the music educator ideas and activities for presenting gospel music lessons in an academic setting, mainly the classroom.

Gospel Music in Schools, Colleges, and Universities

Since the Supreme Court's decision ruling prayer out of schools, many changes have taken place in presenting music with a sacred text in the classroom. For instance, educators are taking precautions in presenting the music, especially on religious holidays such as Easter and other cultural celebrations.

Therefore, gospel music must be taught as an art form in the academic setting. The students clearly understand the background of this music, and will often refer to it themselves as church music. The instructor has the task of proper instructional delivery and keeping the music in its proper context. Many educators were not exposed to gospel in a formal training atmosphere. They were primarily Europe-oriented (meaning that gospel music was not exposed to them in formal training). James Baldwin sums it up in his book, *The Fire Next Time*, when he says:

> *White Americans have supposed "Europe" and "civilization" to be synonyms, which they are not, and have been distrustful of other standards, and other sources of vitality.*

The European concept of music is melody, and the African concept is rhythm. It is upon this point that most white people have difficulty with Negro music, the difficulty of getting the "swing" of it. White America has pretty well mastered this difficulty; and naturally, because the Negro has been beating these rhythms for 300 years.

Many colleges and universities have incorporated music as part of their curriculum. However, there are still some academic institutions that may have gospel as extracurricular or, small groups performing it as only an activity. However, those institutions that have a viable program have reported success through cross-cultural experiences, integrating across the curriculum, community awareness, and knowledge- based experience for life-long learning. The teaching and performance of gospel connects across disciplines, such as Social Studies, English/Language Arts, Technology, Science and other subjects. Research has shown that utilizing the interdisciplinary approach may avoid teaching in isolation. Therefore, skill retention will occur at higher frequency.

Due to the increased demand for more knowledge and performance of gospel music, mostly by students, doors have opened, and academicians are becoming more receptive to this art form. However, one must understand the diverse stylistic trends. Many colleges and universities have applauded their success s in producing high quality performing groups.

In a recent survey taken among college and university students, it was revealed that gospel music on campus proved valuable to them. In summary, it was stated that gospel music was a vehicle sometimes reinforcing values. Some students stated that messages of hope for the future were a spiritual motivation. Campus ministries often incorporate gospel activities, as well as other cross-cultural relations. (Refer to **Student Surveys on Campuses**)

Gospel music education has different meanings to individuals on campus. The impact and influence of gospel is very positive. The Venn Diagram presents some of their thoughts, feelings, and opinions. Students were asked to fill in the vinn-gram regarding the influences of gospel on campus. (See Venn Diagram page 106).

Other positive comments on gospel were:

- "It [performing in Gospel Choir] has been one of the most fulfilling experiences of my life. It has opened many doors for me. I gained travel experience and further developed vocal skills, states Chania Dillard, a graduating Senior.

- "Singing in the college Gospel Choir, which is a performance class, has allowed me understand music in the context of history," states Michelle Brooks, a Junior (2008)

Many performance groups, on and off campus, are mainly focusing on learning repertoire for performances. However, it is of utmost importance to incorporate skills, history, and discipline to the group. Many college students may not be familiar with the historical background of the subject. On campus a large majority of the students only hear that which is available on radio, television and online. When introducing music materials to the group, historical background, intended message, and compositional elements should be shared.

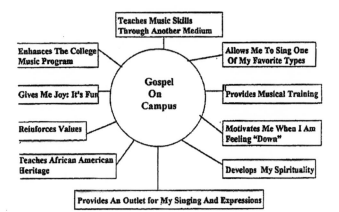

The Significance of African American Music in the Curriculum

a. It provides another avenue for students in terms of career opportunitie(Professional gospel artists, etc.)

b. It broadens one's horizon and understanding of a type of historical music that is heard in a daily basis.

c. It enhances multi-cultural awareness and music appreciatio(not only Afro- American music should be introduced, but also music of other World cultures as well)

d. It creates an awareness of the struggles that went into the making of this great body of music.

e. Exposure will broaden the students' knowledge allowing them to discriminate one type of music from another.

Gospel Music in the Formal Educational Setting

Students readily identify with gospel music. They react spontaneously by moving and clapping as they sing. Gospel music serves as a multi-communicative agent, leading to group interaction along with expression of the literature. Many music skills can be reinforced through gospel music, which affords a built-in success factor.

So, why is gospel music so seldom a part of some music programs?

Gospel music has for many years been considered by the European-oriented musical authorities to be beneath notice, and illegitimate offshoot of sacred music, and certainly was not to be performed in a formal educational setting. Like jazz, ragtime, blues, and other forms of highly emotional music that deals with the heart rather than the intellect, gospel was not even an acceptable topic of academic interest for the professional musicologist in previous decades. There are quite a few institutions that can verify this fact. Times have changed, and today many music educators are achieving desired goals and developing music skills through this medium. Dr. Horace Boyer, writer of the forward to this book, spent a lifetime educating, bringing gospel music into the mainstream and validating it for the analysis and performance of higher education. Unfortunately, there may be some educators who have not fully embraced this music as an art form for many reasons. However, failure to expose this significant body of music to students may have a negative effect on career opportunities for the students.

Due to scholarly interest (researching and composing) in gospel, the music has gained prominence and being performed in places previously denied. Some of these venues include catholic services, cathedrals, theaters, Broadway, and prominent concert halls. In many instances, gospel music is now being incorporated into the instructional plans and music activities for the benefit of students in public schools and colleges. There is a quest for more knowledge of the history and performance techniques of gospel music, especially among those persons who may not have had direct interaction with it previously. Workshops, seminars and conferences are gaining popularity due to this increased interest. More instructional materials are being developed and becoming available to meet the growing demands and challenges of teachers who are eager to share and expose students to gospel music.

Myths about Gospel Music

As a result of many years of training, performing, teaching, conducting gospel music workshops, seminars, and clinics, I have exchanged some interesting views that may further develop and promote positive outcomes in gospel music instructions. The following views or statements may help to eradicate and dispel some common myths of gospel music.

a. **Singing gospel ruins the voice.** One need not sacrifice the level of musical excellence when performing gospel. Of course, any type of music performed without the use of proper vocal techniques will ruin the voic

b. **Gospel music can be sung most effectively by Black performer.** Music has no color line, and no single group has sole claim on this music or other form. However, cultural heritage, or background may be an advantage in effective inter-pretation of gospel styleVarious cultures are participating, singing and performing Black gospel style. There are international groups and chapters of many cultures that are affiliated with gospel music.

c. **Gospel music requires minimum skill.** The complex melodic, rhythmic and harmonic structure of the music requires proficiency in theory, composition, and improvisation (the main ingredient in gospel). Many classical oriented scholars have successfully combined formal training with gospel techniques and produced quality compositions and perfor-mance group.

d. **Gospel music should only be used in religious setting.** Just as the Negro Spiritual was used for communication as well as for religious purposes, so it is with gospel music. Gospel is in the mainstream. Although it is used most often as part of worship services, many individuals employ gospel music as an agent in promoting social educational, spiritual, and moral welfare. Classical religious works are present in the curriculum (Bach, Handel, etc.). So, the same should apply to gospel composers.

Presentation is the Key

Certain principles and practices should be adhered to when presenting gospel music in the formal educational setting.

a. **Do not infringe upon the religious rights of other.** Just as one would present the religious music of Bach or Beethoven (introducing the style and musical elements), the same should apply to gospel music. Teach the music as an art form. Do not teach the doctrine.

b. **Suitable compositions should be a key element when introducing and incorporating gospel as a part of the lesson plan.** Awareness of the instructional population (age group) in terms of vocal ranges and comprehension level is vital. Be in command of interpretation and style of composition.

c. **Adhere to vocal and instrumental performance practice.** Demand proper breath control, diction, and pitch acuity, coordinating phonation with breath, comprehension and interpretation of style, improvisational technique, and theoretical application. Enforce the aesthetics and beauty of singing the music. Do not scream.

d. **Reinforce skills.** Present skills-oriented lessons. Incorporate the transferal of skills acquired via the study of other subjects and facets of music. Present the skills necessary for proficiency in performance, composition, and reading, within the medium of gospel music.

e. **Incorporate gospel with other styles such as blues, jazz, ragtime, and spiritual.** Students may then be able to make and easier comparison of musical elements on relationship to other types of music when skills are not together in isolation. Some compositions can be performed in many different styles ranging form classical to contemporary gospel.

Testimony To Gospel's Effectiveness

Many educators have experienced positive results in skill achievement in music via gospel music. Some of these validations for gospel music's effectiveness are cited.

The late Pearl Williams-Jones, noted gospel performer and faculty member of the University of the District of Columbia, stated that "Gospel music and spirituals deserve their place in the curriculum beside the religious music traditions of other world cultures. Just as the mass, motet, chorales, and anthems have historically been included in the curriculum, so should gospel and spirituals. These, too, should be included among the world's great religious music. Their cultural historical, educational, and spiritual significance is evident."

Susan Waiters-Walls, an experienced elementary school teacher in the Washington D.C. metropolitan area and Prince George's County, Maryland, states that gospel music brings about excitement at the elementary school level. The students readily respond to the rhythms by hand-clapping, taps, swaying and moving to the beat. Many of the lyrics and tunes in the songs are familiar to them due to their activities in local churches. Gospel music is effective for reinforcing and teaching musical elements. Ms. Waiter-Walls recently toured China with a group of students to share our musical culture.

Emory Andrews, prominent music educator, composer, director, and teacher in Prince George's County schools, works with choral and classical music with youth and adults. His Oxon Hill Maryland gospel choir is a winner of a previous Stella Awards competition for "Best Choir of the Year" in children's music division.

He too attests to the fact that through gospel music many skills can be reinforced and obtained. After all, he states that "The Child's Bill of Rights" advocates musical experiences for all children. It is up to the educators to insure that all types of music are being exposed.

Collegiate Gospel

Gospel music is prevalent on all levels in our society from elementary schools to college. The late Dr. Camille Taylor, Black Caucus member and former Music Educator National Conference (MENC) chairperson, spearheaded annual gospel music competitions for many years in New York City. This program consisted of gospel performances from students of elementary, junior, senior, community colleges, and universities. They were performance-based adjudications. The GMWA has hosted Collegiate Night at its annual planning board meetings in March for the preparation of the national convention of GMWA which is held in the late summer. This year, the Collegiate Night, "Gospel Goes to College" has been chaired by Dr. Joan Hillsman since its inception at 1910. This year's Collegiate Night in Los Angeles California included 185 student participating from various institutions, sharing their gospel music with others. Dr. Tanya Egler from Wheaton College, Wheaton Illinois who has twenty-five years of experience with her gospel choir stated that this event is a valuable aspect of coming together with other students across the U.S. Her choir consists of fifty students of diverse cultures, presenting gospel music techniques. They range from spiritual, classical, and other subgenres. Other participants agree to the value of Collegiate Night experiences. Professor LaTonya Wrenn, concert pianist at Bowie State University, combines her classical experiences with gospel compositions. She states that students are able to value their formal training that utilized in gospel music performances as well. She incorporates classical elements within gospel pieces. (Please refer to others in the **Appendix, Classical Concert Pianists** section.)

Use of Technology Enhancements

Due to the rapid growth, accessibility, and changes to technology, many colleges and artists of all genres are able to more readily produce and distribute their work for mass exposure, whether it is in MP3 downloaded files, CDs, online-streamed videos, and assignments posted to web-based class courses. Other laypersons, community organization leaders, and general gospel music enthusiasts who may or may not have training have been able to use multi-media techniques to enhance their growth in gospel music.

VIII. THINGS TO DO IN THE CLASSROOM

Listed below are some suggested units, lessons, and activities that may be used at the College, University or other levels of choice.

1. Plan units on "Black Musicians", "Gospel Music", etc. (One appropriate time for the unit on gospel may be in January, for January 15th is Dr. Martin Luther King, Jr.'s birthday). His last song request was "Precious Lord". Aretha Franklin sang "Precious Lord" at Mahalia Jackson's funeral. "Precious Lord" was written by the Father of Gospel music, Thomas A. Dorsey. The death of the world-famous gospel singer, Mahalia Jackson, was January 27, 1972. Aretha Franklin also sang the song "Precious Lord".

2. Comparative units are very effective. For example, one may desire comparing changes made in songs from spiritual to gospel, hymns to gospel, gospel to rock, or one may even trace a particular song through all of the various styles of music, including contemporary music.

3. Song: "Precious Lord"

    a. Review the life of the composer of the song, Thomas Dorsey, the great gospel pioneer.

    b. Relate the song to Mahalia Jackson and DMartin Luther King Jr.

    c. Listen to a selected recording for musical concepts and variations on interpretation of the composition.

    d. Compare spiritual and gospel versions of the song.

4. Classroom Activities

    a. Select an appropriate "call and response" song.

    b. Choose a leader and have the remainder of the class respond to the leader of the sonYou may use "Certainly Lord", or use some other "call and response" song that has been included (see Figure 7).

5. Develop a Gospel timeline of important events for 1930 to the present. Correlate these events in American history (i.e. tell what was happening in the history at the time if the gospel event).

6. Critique in writing a gospel play, performance documentary, video or movie. (Writing across the curriculum is often required in the curriculum of various jurisdictions).

7. Select a contemporary gospel selection and determine at least three (3) re-occurring rhythmic

patterns that hold the song together. Give the instrumentation.

8. Select spirituals that have hidden meanings and decode them. Students may create their own verse and give a hidden meaning.

Mini-Lesson Plans

Teachers may wish to incorporate values, where permitted, and other educational initiatives (Afro centric, writing, etc.) into their lessons plans so as not to teach in isolation. These mini-lessons or instructional activities will provide instructors of all levels ideas for the classroom. Remember, gospel and African centered lessons should be infused throughout the year.

Mini-Lesson #1

TOPIC: African Music Characteristics

OBJECTIVE: To demonstrate music characteristics from out African Roots (Cross rhythms, Syncopation, Improvisation Call and Response, etc.)

SUGGESTED PROCEDURE: The teacher may engage the students in demonstrating examples of African music characteristics which have filtered throughout our African American Music such as:

    a. **Cross-rhythms** – Divide the class into groups, each group performing a different rhythm simultaneously.

b. **Syncopation** – Engage students in clapping a syncopated rhythmic pattern

c. **Improvisation-** Have students create (Vocal or Instrument) a melodic line, then embellishing or making up patterns as they progress.

d. **Call and Response-** Divide the class into two groupHave one side as the "Call" and the other as the "Response", or "Leader" and "Chorus". (See "Go Down Moses")

Mini-Lesson #2

TOPIC: The Beat, Africa's Pulse

OBJECTIVE: To Engage students in varied rhythmic patterns

SUGGEST PROCEDURE: Teacher should have students execute many different rhythms, via body percussions (Tapping, Clapping, and Movements). The beat is the pulse of Africa.

• Many theory and rhythm drills may be incorporated into the lesson beginning with the heart beat or steady beat.

• Engage students in rhythmic dictations. The teacher may select a spiritual or gospel song with selected rhythms to execute.

Mini-Lesson #3

TOPIC: Slave Songs or Negro Spirituals

OBJECTIVE: To install knowledge of Slave Songs/Negro Spirituals and their origin.

SUGGESTED PROCEDURE: Teacher may choose to open discussion on Mood and Music, Contrasting Moods, etc.

Open discussions in Negro slavery, trials and tribulations, the conditions under which the slaves sang.

Discuss and interpret the meaning of the songs.

Analyze a selected spiritual (i.e., "Sometime I Feel Like a Motherless Child") for lyrics, melody, etc.

Mini-Lesson #4

TOPIC: Prominent Spiritual Pioneers

OBJECTIVE: To expose students to the great contributors to the Negro Spiritual.

SUGGESTED PROCEDURE: This activity may take place through a listening or research presentation.

Teacher may have the students do library research on the lives of such musicians as Marian Anderson, Nathaniel Dett, Harry T. Burleigh, Paul Robeson, Roland Hayes, William Dawson, J. Rosamond Johnson, the Fisk Jubilee Singers, and other artists who performed or made contributions to the spirituals (keeping in mind that many of our African American artists included spirituals as a part of their performance repertoire: Jessye Norman, the Author's college room-mate, Leontyne Price, Denise Grave and others.)

Listening Appreciation-Engage the students in listening activities of the various artists and cultural styles.

Mini-Lesson #5

TOPIC: Civil Rights and the Spiritual

OBJECTIVE: To relate how music can be used as a medium of protest.

SUGGESTED PROCEDURE: Discuss the value of music to Dr. Martin Luther King Jr., Civil Rights Leader, and the role that spiritual and gospel music played during the Civil Rights Movement.

Engage the students in singing and interpreting the protest message in some of the songs (i.e., "If You Miss Me").

Mini-Lesson #6

TOPIC: Gospel Music and Its Origin.

OBJECTIVE: To trace the historical development of gospel music from spirituals to the contemporary ere.

SUGGESTED PROCEDURE: The teacher may have the students compare spiritual and gospel music characteristics by construction a comparison chart.

EXAMPLE:

Spiritual	Gospel
Born and developed during slavery	Became popular after the decline of slavery.
More introverted (inward) Simple melody,	Extroverted (moving outward) May be complex in rhythm
	May incorporate much Instrumentation, especially contemporary
Harmony, rhythm (I, IV, V harmony Instrumentation not dominant	

Mini-Lesson #7

TOPIC: Music Composition of Spiritual and Gospel

OBJECTIVE: To compose a selection of the students' choice in one of the styles (spiritual or gospel, traditional or contemporary).

SUGGESTED PROCEDURE: Discuss the various stylistic trends of music, characteristics, etc. and have students compose for that medium.

Mini-Lesson #8

TOPIC: Listening: Classical composers who used Negro thematic materials in their classical compositions.

OBJECTIVE: To be able to analyze or trace the development of the Negro spirituals in classical music.

SUGGESTED PROCEDURE: Have the class listen to the following compositions, picking out the spiritual or folk idioms in each composition: have the class list the title of each Negro work heard.

1. George W. Chadwick- Symphony #2 (the Scherzo shows definite traces of a plantation melody).

2. Antonin Dvorak-

   a. Symphony in E Minor, O95 ("From the New World");

   b. Quartet in F major, O96;

   c. Quintet in E major, O97

3. Frederick Delius- "Appalachia" (a theme and variations on an old slave song for full chorus).

4. Daniel Gregory Mason-String Quartet on Negro Themes, Op. 9 (published in 1919; quotes spirituals for its themes, e.g., "You May bury Me in the East", "Deep River", "Shine, Shine, I'll Meet You in the Morning", "Deep River" repeated, and "Oh, Holy Land."

Mini-Lessons #9

TOPIC: Listening: Negro Composers Who Used Negro Thematic Materials in Classical Compositions.

OBJECTIVE: To develop an appreciation of the Negro's contribution and use of his own music.

SUGGESTED PROCEDURE: Have the class listen to the works of the following composers, picking out the Negro themes in each composition:

1. Clarence Cameron White (arranged spirituals, thematic material, violinist and composer).

2. Samuel Coleridge Taylor (Negro thematic material in his "Twenty-four Negro Melodies" for the piano).

3. William Grant Still (the first symphonic composer among Negro musicians). His larger works include the Afro American Symphony.

4. William Levi Dawson (director of the Tuskegee Choir arranged spirituals for many years). Used Negro themes exclusively. One symphonic effort-Negro Symphony; consisted of arrangements of spirituals for chorus.

5. Harry T. Burleigh (arranged spirituals. Listen to some of these arrangements.

Mini-Lesson #10

TOPIC: Historical Periods in Gospel.

OBJECTIVE: To trace the major developmental stages and periods in gospel music.

SUGGESTED PROCEDURE: The teacher may have the students study the historical developments in gospel music by periods.

1. Have students name major music personalities in various periods who contributed to the field of gospel.

2. Have students cite major works that marked a turning point in gospel.

Mini-Lesson #11

TOPIC: Form and Analysis

OBJECTIVE: To analyze the form of a selected gospel composition.

SUGGESTED PROCEDURE: The teacher may engage the students in two different gospel selections, chart the harmonic progressions, analyze and compare (i.e. a traditional gospel arrangement vs. a contemporary gospel). Use appropriate theory markings and fundamentals in analysis.

Mini-Lesson #12

TOPIC: Gospel Music: A Fusion of African American Music Forms.

OBJECTIVE: To distinguish blues, jazz, ragtime, and other African American music elements infused in gospel.

SUGGESTED PROCEDURE: Have the students select gospel songs which employ characteristics of other African American music forms. Discuss the peculiar characteristics for each style, as well as common elements.

Mini-Lesson #13

TOPIC: Gospel Music in the Religious Setting

OBJECTIVE: To discuss the development of gospel music in the church setting.

SUGGESTED PROCEDURE: Have the students trace the developments of gospel music in the African American church.

Have students listen to varied artists who perform predominantly in the churches (church choirs who are recording artists, etc.) Discuss the gospel artists' techniques and performances styles. Identify improvisational lines and utterances.

Mini-Lesson #14

TOPIC: 21st Century Contemporary Gospel Artists

OBJECTIVE: To survey and list composers and artists who write and perform gospel.

SUGGESTED PROCEDURE: Have students list recent artists who have contributed to this era. Listen to selected compositions by several artists and write about their style of composition.

Lesson Plan Development

Other Topics from Which Lesson Plans May be Developed

- Research and analyze artists and composers whose compositions combine classical elements in gospel music (i.e. Richard Smallwood, LaTonya Wrenn, etc.)

- Research, listen, and compare traditional and contemporary gospel music selections.

- Watch video recordings of various styles of gospel music, plays and performances (i.e. Say Amen Somebody, National Collegiate Gospel Choir Competition, etc.)

- Assign specific shows to watch on television which pertain to gospel music (i.e. BET, TBN, GMC, etc.)

- Report on the lives and music of prominent gospel artists, such as Thomas A. Dorsey, Mahalia Jackson, and others as listed throughout this text.

- Report on crossover artists, such as Sam Cooke, Lou Rawls, Donny Hathaway, and many others.

Summary

Gospel music should be listened to, discussed and taught. This music form is a vital part of the African American culture. It crosses all barriers. For the general enthusiast, it is informative and inspirational. For those in areas of academic research and study, "teaching the content of gospel," not the doctrine, is one of the key elements in presentation. This music should be integrated into the total curriculum and presented with excellent quality.

Gospel music is in the mainstream of all cultures. Multi-ethnic groups incorporate the music characteristics in many settings. Gospel music is often referred to as "The Good News Music," based on the four gospels in the bible: Matthew, Mark, Luke, and John. The fact is, without denial, it is a religious music that has impacted on global art forms. Gospel music has come a long way. Times have changed and it is being recognized on local, national, and international levels. One commentator from the book The Progress of Gospel Music referred to it as beneath academic acceptance. The basic forms of gospel music are traditional and contemporary. However, there are many sub-genres such as gospel reggae, hip-hop gospel, jazz gospel, and so on. These genres incorporate characteristics that create fusions and blending of the music. The availability of media, research, and performances has created a larger stage for its work, causing it to be in the mainstream. The forerunner of gospel originates from the African characteristics, transitioning from spiritual to contemporary gospel. History has provided avenues for greater understanding of this heritage. Spirituals were born during slavery and gospel came on the scene in 1930 with Thomas A. Dorsey who was proclaimed as the "Father of Gospel music." Other pioneers, along with Dorsey, are Charles Tindley (1851-1933), Sally Martin (1896-1988), Mahalia Jackson (1911-1972), Clara Ward (1924-1973), Roberta Martin (1907-1969), Sister Rosetta Tharpe (1915-1973), Rev. James Cleveland (1932-1991), Mattie Moss-Clark (1925-1994), The Five Blind Boys of Alabama, and Albertina Walker (1929-2010) who organized the Caravans consisting of Inez Andrews, Shirley Caeser, James Cleveland, Dorothy Norwood, Cassietta George, and Bessie Griffin. She retired the group in the late 1960s and continued her successful solo career, winning her first Grammy award in 1995.

In 1969, Edward Hawkins bridged the gap from traditional gospel to contemporary gospel with his recording of "Oh Happy Day." This song swept across the globe. I remember being in Paris, France, one New Year's Eve and the band was playing the tune in a secular style for the music. The melody had transcended on an international level. The rendition was incorporated much instrumentation with various complex musicality.

To the young fledging and mature artists, late bloomers coming in the field of gospel and moving into the gospel industry and arena, I have this message: Continue to learn more about gospel and share its heritage and contributions to all cultures in the world of music.

Appendix

Discography

There is a rapid turn-over in the gospel recording industry. Individual groups and artists are recording CD's, cassettes, videos, MP3's on gospel music. Local artists are constantly evolving in various cities around the world. Artists of all ages are exploring ways and means of recording, producing themselves, and even entering into the business of music and recording industry. Technological advances have enhanced these opportunities even from a grass-roots level. This listing of artists may serve as a guide for traditional, contemporary and other specific genres in gospel. It is not, by all means, a complete account of all who have contributed to this body of music. The discography (list of recordings) of each may be obtained from selected resources and collections.

List of Artists

Traditional

Angelic Gospel Singers
Andrews, Inez
Allen, Rance & Group
Armstrong, Vanessa Bell
Banks, Bishop Jeff
Barnes, Rev. F.C. & Janice
Barrett Singers
Bignon, James
Boyer Brothers
(Drs. Horace and James)
Bradford, Alex
Caesar, Shirley
Cage, Byron
Clark Sisters
Clark, Mattie Moss
Clark, Mildred
Cleveland, Rev. James
Coates, Dorothy Love
Dixon, Rev. Jessie
Dorsey, Thomas A.
Drinkard Family
Evans, Rev. Clay
Ford, Charles & Singers
George, Cassietta
Houston, Cissy
Jackson, Mahalia
Jakes, Rev. TD & Singers
Martin, Sallie
May, Joe

Miller, Douglas
Moore, James
Norwood, Dorothy
O'Neal Twins (Edgar & Eddie)
Pearson, Carlton
Peoples, Dottie
Rasberry, Raymond
Robinson, Cleophus
Staples Singers
Sumners, Myrna
Truthettes
Vails, Donald
Ward Singers
Walker, Albertina

Contemporary

Adams, Yolanda
Brooklyn Tabernacle
Burrell, Kim
Carr, Kurt
Clark Sisters
Clark-Sheard, Karen
Coley, Daryl
Commissioned
Crouch, Andre
Crouch, Sandra
Franklin, Kirk
God's Property
Green, Al
Haddon, Deidrick
Hall, Danibelle
Hairston, J.

Hammond, Fred
Hawkins, Edwin
Hawkins Family
Hawkins, Tramaine
Hawkins, Walter
Hayes, Craig
Houghton, Israel
Kee, John P.
Lawrence, Donald
Majors, Jeff
Manuzzi, Martha
McClurkin, Donnie
Morrison, Nathaniel ("God Is")
Moss, Jay
Munuzzi, Martha
Norful, Smokie
Pace, LaShaun
Phipps, Whitley
Smallwood, Richard
Tribett, Tye
Trotter, Bishop Larry
Whitman, Walt
Whitfield, Thomas
Winans Family (Bebe & Cece)
Walker, Hezikiah
Whitman, Walt
Whitfield, Thomas
Wright, Timothy
Yohi, Vicki
Youthful Praise

Quartets

Blind Boys of Alabama (5)
Blind Boys of Mississippi (5)
Brooklyn All-Stars
Canton Spirituals
Dixie Hummingbirds
Fairfield Four
Fountain, Clarence
Golden Gates
Gospel Keynotes
Harmonizing Four
Jackson Southernaires
Jeter, Claude
Mighty Clouds of Joy
Pilgrim Jubilees
Nightingales
Soul Stirrers
Swan Silvertones
Williams Brothers

Recording Mass Choirs

Alaska Mass Choir
Chicago Mass Choir
Evans, Rev. Clay
Florida Mass Choir
Full Gospel Baptist Mass Choir
Georgia Mass Choir
Gospel Music Workshop of America Mass Choirs (GMWA)
(Recording Departments: Youth, Women, Men, National
Mass)
Mississippi Children's Choir

Mississippi Mass Choir
New Generation (Ricky Dillard)
Soul Children of Chicago
Soul Children of New Orleans
Thompson Community Choir
Wilmington Chester Mass Choir

College & University Gospel Choirs

(Many institutions have specific gospel choir groups, while others incorporate gospel and other genres such as spirituals in regular choral programs)

American University Gospel Choir (Washington, D.C.)
Binghamton College (Binghamton, NY)
Bowie State University Gospel Choir
Cortland College Gospel Choir (Cortland, NY)
Florida A&M (Tallahassee, Florida)
Florida State
Georgetown University Gospel Choir (D.C.)
Hampton University (Hampton, Virginia)
Howard University Gospel Choir
Morgan State University
Syracuse University (Black Celestrial Choir)
University of Toledo
Virginia State University
Virginia Union

Classical Concert Pianists

(Some classical concert artists also incorporate gospel compositions in their performance arrangements. Listed here are a few)

Cason, Minister Daniel
Cureton, Evelyn
Joi-Morgan, Dana Kristina
Jones, (late) Pearl-Williams
Joubert, Joseph
Smallwood, Richard
Wrenn, LaTonya

Index of Names

Dett, Nethaniel
Dixie, Hummingbirds
Dixon, Jesse
Dorsey, Thomas A.
Fields, Dr. Peter
Fisk Jubilee Singers
Fold, Charles
Franklin, Aretha
Franklin, Kirk
Gospel Harmonettes
Hall, Danniebelle
Hammond, Fred
Hathaway, Donny
Harmonizing Four
Hawkins, Edwin
Hawkins, Singers
Jackson, Rev. Jesse
Jackson, Mahalia
Johnson, J. Rosamond
Johnson, James Weldon
Jones, Pearl Williams
Jones, Ron
Kee, John P.
King, Martin Luther, Jr.
LaBelle, Patty
Lawrence, Donald
Martin, Roberta
Martin, Sally
Mary Mary
May, Brother Joe
McClurkin, Donnie
McLin, Lena
Mighty Clouds of Joy
Moss, J.

Norwood, Dorothy
Pilgrim Jubilees
Payton, Ricky
Preston, Billy
Rainey, Ma
Rawls, Lou
Robeson, Paul
Sapp, Marvin
Smallwood, Richard
Smith, Rev. Bennett
Smith, Bessie
Smith, Mamie
Soul Stirrers
Staple Singers
Summers, Myrna
Take Six
Tharpe, Rosetta
Tye Tribbett & G.A.
Utterbach, Clinton
Walker, Albertina
Walker, Hezekiah
Ward, Clara
Watts, Isaac
Williams, Ophelia
Winans Family
Work, John

Gospel Resources & Organizations

(These available resources and organizations may be utilized to assist you in pursuing more information in the field of gospel music, research, business of music and other general needs. Contact information may be found on websites via internet, google searches and networks. Also, please use these search tools for other artists, listings, and cultural sub-genres that might not included in this compilation.)

- The Gospel Music Workshop of America, Inc.

- (GMWAnational.net)

- The Edwin Hawkins Music & Arts

- The Thomas A. Dorsey Convention of Choirs and Choruses

- BET Network with Dr. Bobby Jones (TV) Listings

- Joan Hillsman's Music Network, Inc. (JHMN)

- P.O. Box 83, Syracuse, New York 13205, additional contacts:

- (email: jhillsman@twcny.rr.com), Phone: 315-373-0805. www.joan hillam.com)

- National Association for Music Education, NAFME), Reston, Virginia, formerly

- known as MENC). This Organization sets the standards for the arts in the schools

- and education in general.

- It's God's Choice Religious Bookstore (Sheet Music, robes, and church ministry,

- Accessories)

- N'Time Music, Charlotte, N.C.

- Sacred Melody Bookstore, Syracuse, New York

- Dales Music Store, Silver Springs, Maryland

- Library of Congress (Washington, D. C.) –
  Copyright Registrations, Patents, etc.

- BMI, ASCAP (Royalties, Registered Works)

- Billboard (Ratings)

- Gospel Music Industry Round Up (Lisa Collins,
  Eye on Gospel Publications)

- (Provide contacts for artists,, churches, email
  marketing, websites and more.

- Gospel Hall of Fame

- Stella Awards

- National Association for Negro Musicians
  (NANM Organization)

- Gospel Announcers Guild (GMWA

- Church Music Workshops and general presenta-
  tions, music and educational

Materials, available through Dr. Joan Hillsman's Music
Network, Inc.

Special Documentary Videos:

- "Say Amen, Somebody"

- BET special: "Joyful Noise" featuring Latifah

- "A Spiritual Journey Documenting The Life of
  Harriet Tubman by Dr. Joan Hillsman & Syracuse

Chapter of GMWA) (Inquire: CD available along with story of The Underground Railroad,

Email: jhillsman@twcny.rr.com

Website: http://joanhillsmanmusicnetwork.com/

For all of your music needs network with Dr. Joan Hillsman's Music Network, Inc.

Bibliography

Allen, Williams, Charles, Lucy Garrison, Slave Songs of the United States. New York: Peter Smith, 1951.

Baker, Barbara Wesley, Black Gospel Music Styles. Ph.D. Dissertation, Baltimore: University of Maryland, 1978.

Boatner, Edward, The Story of the Spirituals. Miami: Belwin Mills, 1973.

Bontempts, Arna, Chariot In the Sky: A story of the Jubilee Singers. New York: New York: Holt, Rinehart and Winston, 1971.

Broughton, Viv, Black Gospel: An Illustrated History of the Gospel Sound. New York: Poole, Dorset, Blandford Press,1985.

Bowman, Sister Thea, "The Gift of African American Sacred Song". Chicago: The African American Catholic Journal, GIA Publication, 1987.

Boyer, Horace C.,The Gospel Song: An Historical and Analytical Survey. Masters Thesis, New York: Eastman School of Music, University of Rochester, 1964.

_____, How Sweet The Sound: The Golden Age of Gospel. Washington, D.C.: Elliott & Clark. Inquiries: E&C Publishers, P.O. Box 21038, Washington, D.C. 20009.

Carawan, Guy and Candi, Sing for Freedom: The Story of the Civil Rights Movement Through Its Songs. Pennsylvania: Sing Out Corp., 1990.

Courlander, Harold, Negro Folk Music. USA, New York: Columbia University Press, 1963.

Cone, James H., The Spiritual and the Blues. New York: Seabury Press, 1972.

Cusic, Don, The Sound of Light: A History of Gospel. Bowling Green: Bowling Green State University Press, 1990

Dett, Nathaniel R. (ed.), Religious Folk Songs of the Negro. New York: AMS Press, 1972.

DeLerma, Dononique-Rene, Reflections on Afro-American Music. Ohio State University Press, 1973.

Dubois, W.E.B., The Souls of Black Folk. New York: Bantan Books, 1989.

Dupree, Sherry and Herbert, African American Good News. Washington, D.C.: Mid-Atlantic Regional Press, 1993.

Fisher, Miles M., Negro Slave Songs In The United States. New York: Russell and Russell, 1968.

George, Luvenia A., Teaching The Music Of Six Different Cultures. Danbury, Connecticut: World Music Press, 1990.

Hillsman, Joan R.,The Progress of Gospel Music: From Spirituals To Contemporary Gospel. (Contact JHMN, P.O. Box 83, Syracuse, New York, 13205)

_____, Sequential Instructional Plans for Administering Gospel Music Lessons In The Classroom," PhD Dissertation, The Union Institute & University, Cincinnati, Ohio, 1978.

_____, Gospel Music: An African American Art Form. McGraw Hill, 1998, ISBN 0-07-154037-7, 1st ed.

_____, The Church Music Ministry Series, Available through JHMN, Inc., 2014. (email jhillsman@twcny.rr.com)

Hillsman, Quentin J., The Art of Playing The Tambourine. Available Through JHMNm Inc.

Heilbut, Anthony, The Gospel Sound. New York: Anchor Press Doubleday, 1985.

Johnson, James Weldon and J. Rosamond, The Book of American Negro Spirituals, 2 Vols., New York: Dacapo Press. 1973.

Jones, Arthur C., Wade In The Water: Wisdom of the Spiritual. New York: Orbis Books, 1993.

Kemp, Kathryn B., Make A Joyful Noise: A Brief History of Gospel Music Ministry in America. Chicago: Joyful Noise Press, 2011.

Nketia, J.H. Kwabena, The Music Of Africa. New York: W.W. Norton, 1974.

Patterson, Lindsay, International Library of Negro Life and History. New The Association of Negro Life and

History. New York: The Association For The Study Of Negro Life and History, 1967.

Reagan-Johnson, Bernice, We'll Understand It Better By and By. Washington, D. C.: Smithsonian Institution Press, 1992.

Roach, Hildred, Black American Music: Past and Present, 2d Ed.), Florida: Krieger Publishers, 1992.

Southern, Eileen, The Music of Black Americans (2d ED,), New York: W.W. Norton, 1983.

Spencer, Jon Michael, Protest and Praise:Sacred Music of Black Religion. Minnesota: Augsbury Fortress, 1990.

Walker, Wyatt T., Somebody's Calling My Name. Valley Forge: Judson Press, 1979.

Warren, Lee, The Music of Africa. Englewood Cliffs: Prentice Hall, Inc., 1970.

Choral Arrangement of Spirituals

"Elijah Rock"-Jester Hairston

"Daniel, Daniel Servant of The Lord"-Undine Moore

"Ride the Chariot"-Henry Smith

"Ain't Got Time to Die"-Hall Johnson/G Schrimer Pub.

"Witness"-Hall Johnson

"Lily Of The Valley"-Wendell Whalen

"Let Us Break Bread Together"-Noah Ryder

"Come Here Jesus"-Verolga Nix

"I Know The Lord Laid His hand On Me"-Jefferson Cleveland

"Give Me Jesus"- Verolga Nix

Additional References-Selections by Nolan Williams, Evelyn White collections, Evelyn Cureton and others.

Liner Notes

The knowledge of the education, relevance, and history of gospel music is absolutely essential as a part of our cultural heritage. This body of knowledge is of utmost importance.

Ron Jones
Music Consultant
University of Louisville
and National Radio Consultant

Congratulations on such a valuable contribution to the field of gospel music,

Dr. Rodena Preston.
Renowned Pianist Director and Composer
Minister of Music for the
Gospel Music Workshop of America, Inc.
(GMWA)

This is an invaluable contribution from Dr. Horace Boyer in the perpetuation of gospel music at a higher level of education.

Dr. James Boyer
Retired Professor of Music
Manhattan, Kansas

About the Author

Joan Rucker-Hillsman, a native of Anderson, South Carolina, received a Bachelor of Music Education and Masters of Music Education degrees from Howard University, matriculated at Catholic University of America in the Doctor of Music Arts program, and received a Ph.D in Musicology from The Union Institute & University, Cincinnati, Ohio. Her Doctoral Dissertation was on "Sequential Instructions for Administering Gospel Music in an Academic Setting". Dr. Hillsman is a lecturer, performer, composer and a well-known Church Music Consultant with international recognition. She is also an author of several books, including the second edition of this revised compilation, "Gospel Music: An African American Art Form", McGraw Hill Publisher. She is on the National Board of Directors of the James Cleveland Gospel Music Workshop of America (GMWA), served in the Academic Division as S Scholarship Chairperson, and currently chairs the National Collegiate Night: "Gospel Goes to College", a program which was proposed and established by her. She has worked on the college/university level serving on Doctoral committees for several institutions of higher education. She worked on a project, "African American Music Concepts" at Harvard University with the late renowned professor, Eileen Southern.

Dr. Hillsman retired as Supervising Director of Music for all of the D. C. Public Schools (1996), and was appointed Professor of Music and Director of the Bowie State University Gospel Choir. She has served in several capacities of Music Ministry, as a consultant and Minister of Music. Her travels have taken her to London, Paris, Spain, Alex Haley's Village (Jufuru in Senegar-The Gambia), Sweden and many other places. Her community services are too numerous to mention. However, she holds the "Key to the City of Detroit", Michigan (presented by the late Mayor Coleman Young), listed in several Marquis Directories, "Who's Who in Education, Who's Who in the World", to name a few of its entries. In Washington, D.C. she received a "Neighborhood Grant", which resulted in Joan Hillsman's Day in the Nation's Capital, awarded by former Mayor Marion Barry, and received accolades for forming the "D.C.'s First Gospel Homeless Choir". She is a member of Phi Delta Kappa, Gamma Sigma Sigma, Sigma Alpha Iota, and Alpha Kappa Alpha Sorority. She served as co-chair for the First National Historically Black College and University (HBCU) Conductor's Summit at the John F. Kennedy Center in 2008 under Toni Roy, Project Director. Dr. Hillsman is a member of MENC, Music Education National Conference, currently renamed National Association for Music Education (NAFME), headquartered in Reston, Virginia.

Dr. Hillsman relocated to Syracuse, New York in 2010 and continued her advocacy for the arts and community volunteering. She worked on the "Say Yes to Education" program served as clinician for its Summer Institute, serves on the Annual Dr. Martin Luther King, Jr. Program, Hendricks Chapel Annual Concerts, works on Harriet Tubman Projects, served on Mayor Stephanie Miner's Arts Transitional Team, and her Women's Commission. She is currently the CEO of

Joan Hillsman's Music Network, Inc. (JHMN). She has one son, Quentin Hillsman, Head Women's Basketball Coach at Syracuse University.

CPSIA information can be obtained at www.ICGtesting.com
Printed in the USA
LVOW12*1516080415

433774LV00004B/43/P

9 781460 232194